ESTRENO Collection of Contemporary Spanish Plays

General Editor: Phyllis Zatlin

THE SIEGE OF LENINGRAD

JOSÉ SANCHIS SINISTERRA

THE SIEGE OF LENINGRAD
(A Story Without End)

(*El cerco de Leningrado:
Historia sin final*)

Translated from the Spanish
by
Mary-Alice Lessing

ESTRENO Plays
New Brunswick, New Jersey
2003

ESTRENO Contemporary Spanish Plays 24
General Editor: Phyllis Zatlin
Department of Spanish & Portuguese
Faculty of Arts & Sciences
Rutgers, The State University of New Jersey
105 George Street
New Brunswick, New Jersey 08901-1414 USA

Library of Congress Cataloging in Publication Data
Sanchis Sinisterra, José, 1940-
The Siege of Leningrad
Bibliography:
Contents: The Siege of Leningrad
Translation of: El cerco de Leningrado.
1. Sanchis Sinisterra, José, 1940-
Translation, English.
I. Lessing, Mary-Alice. II. Title.
Library of Congress Control No.: 2003104937
ISBN: 1-888463-16-3

The publishers wish to acknowledge
financial assistance for this translation from the
Dirección General del Libro, Archivos y Bibliotecas
del Ministerio de Educación, Cultura y Deporte de España

Cover: Jeffrey Eads

Judith Magre and Emmanuelle Riva in *Le Siège de Leningrad* (*The Siège of Leningrad*). Colline National Theatre, Paris, 1997. Dir. Dominique Poulange. Photo by Laurencine Lot.

A NOTE ON THE PLAY

Two old actresses reside in an abandoned theatre called The Ghost Playhouse. They have learned that the building will soon be destroyed to make way for a ramp to a parking garage. At first they are simply engaged in finding what remains of their past. The theatre had been home to their socialist collective dedicated to Marxist principles. But it had been closed after the mysterious death of the company's leading actor, Nestor, who had been married to one of the women and was having an affair with the other. Priscilla, the wife, holds no grudges against Natalie; their focus now is on finding ways to preserve the theatre, their past, and their socialist ideals. As they rummage through the memorabilia and old costumes, they gradually unravel secrets from their history they had not known. When they unearth a copy of *The Siege of Leningrad*, the play their company was producing when it closed, their memories and their realities are shattered forever.

Each of the women is intiguing and compelling. They are complex characters in spite of the fact that we learn virtually nothing about their lives outside the theatre. They hold meetings to admit past and current mistakes, but there are never recriminations or any sense of deep regret. At times they confront each other about the past; at other times, they confront their own memories. Their commitment to the political principles of the theatre company gave them the strength to accept Nestor's infidelities; it now carries them through the final revelation they could never have believed.

The Siege of Leningrad is a remarkable blend of theatrical styles. The two women behave quite normally as they sift through their theatre's history. They construct a realistic narrative of the theatre that gave them their purpose and of their love for Nestor as young women in the postwar years. Much of their dialogue is matter-of-fact and normal. Yet they also wander through a surrealistic landscape of old fantasies, nightmares, and partial truths. Sometimes they banter in dialogue that they remember directly from their past; at other times, each faces the empty theatre to confess and reveal her hidden memories. Like Vladimir and Estragon in *Waiting for Godot*, they often seem helpless, lost, and as abandoned as The Ghost Playhouse. Often they are trapped in a postmodern conundrum, in which the truth of the past destroys all of their constructions of the reality they have clung to for so many years. Yet in the end, their Marxist determination to overcome their oppressors seems to pull them back to a reality they will face regardless of the consequences. *The Siege of Leningrad* is a beautifully written text filled with rich theatricality and mesmerizing stage moments.

Grant McKernie
Professor of Theatre
University of Oregon

JOSÉ SANCHIS SINISTERRA
Photo by Phyllis Zatlin

ABOUT THE PLAYWRIGHT

José Sanchis Sinisterra, born in Valencia in 1940, is one of the most respected contemporary playwrights of the Spanish language. He is also a distinguished director, theoretician and teacher. In this latter capacity, he is widely recognized for his outstanding service as mentor for numerous younger playwrights.

Since age seventeen, when Sanchis Sinisterra began writing and directing, his work has been characterized by a passionate quest to explore the frontiers of theatricality and societal norms. Early in his career, he founded and directed independent theatre groups. In 1971, he became a professor at the Theatre Institute in Barcelona, where he founded the experimental Teatro Fronterizo. In 1989, he became director of the Sala Beckett, the new headquarters of the Teatro Fronterizo. As a director, Sanchis Sinisterra has staged works by Sophocles, Cervantes, Shakespeare, Pirandello, Brecht and Beckett, among others. He has likewise directed his own works, in Spain and abroad, and has been the recipient of numerous awards, including Spain's National Theatre Prize. He has penned more than thirty-five original plays and adaptations.

Sanchis Sinisterra defends a "minor-key" theatricality, distinct from commercial spectacle and populated by characters at the margins of power. His formal elements include metatheatre, minimalist staging, humor and pathos, the juxtaposition of realism and fantasy, temporal and spatial ruptures, and a hybridization of epic, comic, narrative and dramatic forms and linguistic registers.

Early works, such as *Demasiado frío* (Too Much Cold, 1965) and *Testigo de poco* (Worthless Witness, 1973), evince Brechtian social realism and political critique. *La leyenda de Gilgamesh* (The Legend of Gilgamesh, 1977) initiates his investigation of theatricality. His first major success, *Ñaque o de piojos y actores* (Two-Man Company or About Lice and Actors, 1980), is a metatheatrical study of theatre and the human condition that reveals the influence of Beckett.

Historical revisionism shapes his trilogy on the Spanish conquest of the Americas and his examination of the Spanish Civil War, *¡Ay, Carmela!* (1986). His best-known work internationally, *¡Ay, Carmela!* has been made into a movie (1990, dir. Carlos Saura) and performed in English in Great Britain. Also among his most successful works is *El lector por horas* (The Hired Reader, 1999).

Ñaque, ¡Ay, Carmela! and *El cerco de Leningrado* (*The Siege of Leningrad*, 1994), comprise the author's "trilogy of the empty stage." *The Siege of Leningrad* refers metaphorically to the fall of the Berlin Wall. It has been performed to acclaim in Spain, Argentina, Mexico and France.

Linda Materna
Rider University

Inquiries regarding permissions should be addressed to the author through

D. Alfredo Carrión Saiz
Director de Artes Escénicas y Musicales
Sociedad General de Autores y Editores
Fernando VI, 4
28004 Madrid, SPAIN
Phone: 011-34-91-349-96-86   Fax: 011-34-91-349-97-12
E-mail: acarrion@sgae.es

or through the translator:

Mary-Alice Lessing
27 Marion Road
Princeton, NJ 08540
Phone: 1-609-924-3534
E-mail: tkless@aol.com

El cerco de Leningrado (Historia sin final) had its premiere on 10 March 1994 at the Teatro Barakaldo in Bilbao, Spain. It was directed by Omar Grasso, with set design by Toni Cortés. Nuria Espert appeared in the role of Natalia and María Jesús Valdés in the role of Priscila. Following a tour that included various cities throughout Spain as well as Buenos Aires, Argentina, *El cerco de Leningrado* in October 1994 reached Madrid, where it was performed at the María Guerrero National Theatre.

Le Siège de Leningrad (Histoire sans fin) (translated by Ángeles Muñoz) was performed at the Colline National Theatre in Paris 3 May to 22 June 1997. The French production was directed by Dominique Poulange and starred Judith Magre as Natalia and Emmanuelle Riva as Priscila.

THE CHARACTERS

NATALIE
PRISCILLA
   (Both women are getting on in years.)

THE SCENE

A vacant theatre.

THE TIME

After the fall.

ACT I

SCENE 1

The lights in the theatre go out. In the darkness one hears the voice of PRISCILLA coming from above the stage.

PRISCILLA'S VOICE: What's happening? *(Silence.)* Natalie! What's happening? *(Silence.)* Natalie! Are you there?
NATALIE'S VOICE *(Far off)*: Yes!
PRISCILLA'S VOICE: What's happened?
NATALIE'S VOICE: Priscilla!
PRISCILLA'S VOICE: What?
NATALIE'S VOICE: The lights have gone out!
PRISCILLA'S VOICE: I'm aware of that, idiot! Do you think I'm blind?
NATALIE'S VOICE: The lights have gone out!
PRISCILLA'S VOICE: I'm not deaf either! Where are you?
NATALIE'S VOICE: The lights, I said.
PRISCILLA'S VOICE: Did you touch the switchboard? *(Silence.)* Natalie!
NATALIE'S VOICE: I'm coming, I'm coming!
PRISCILLA'S VOICE: Where are you going? What are you doing?
NATALIE'S VOICE: There are no lights!
PRISCILLA'S VOICE: No! Really!
NATALIE'S VOICE: Priscilla!
PRISCILLA'S VOICE: What?
NATALIE'S VOICE: Can you hear me, Priscilla?
PRISCILLA'S VOICE: I hear you just fine!
NATALIE'S VOICE: Priscilla!
PRISCILLA'S VOICE: Yes, what is it?
NATALIE'S VOICE: Whatever you do, don't move. Watch out you don't fall. Is the railing steady?
PRISCILLA'S VOICE: Yes.
NATALIE'S VOICE: Can you hear me, Priscilla? I'm here in the dressing rooms, looking for a kerosene lamp.
PRISCILLA'S VOICE: A what?
NATALIE'S VOICE: A kerosene lamp! Because the lights have gone out. Be careful of that railing.
PRISCILLA'S VOICE: There's one in the second dressing room!
NATALIE'S VOICE: What?
PRISCILLA'S VOICE: In the second room there's one!
NATALIE'S VOICE: One what?

PRISCILLA'S VOICE: A kerosene lamp! Watch out for that pitcher of Mari-Gaila's!

(There is the sound of china falling and breaking.)

NATALIE'S VOICE: What did you say? I can't hear you very well.
PRISCILLA'S VOICE: Nothing, nothing at all. Did you hurt yourself?
NATALIE'S VOICE: Priscilla!
PRISCILLA'S VOICE: What?
NATALIE'S VOICE: Do you know what I found in the second dressing room?
PRISCILLA'S VOICE *(Sarcastically)*: Don't tell me. See if I can guess.
NATALIE'S VOICE: Mari-Gaila's pitcher! *(Pause.)* I've got it!
PRISCILLA'S VOICE: What have you got?
NATALIE'S VOICE: Priscilla, I found it! Let's see if I can get it lighted.
PRISCILLA'S VOICE: Be careful with Doña Rosita's costumes. They're so filmy! *(Silence.)* Do you hear me, Natalie? *(Silence.)* Natalie!

(NATALIE enters from the wings lighting her way with a kerosene lamp. She is wearing a cleaning smock and a kerchief over her hair.)

NATALIE: It really gets to me when I go into that dressing room. *(She lifts up the lamp and speaks to someone overhead.)* You know that, Priscilla? Are you up there?
PRISCILLA'S VOICE *(In a bad mood)*: No, I swung down on the ropes, like Tarzan.
NATALIE: It's like that every time I go into that dressing room, and it's even worse when it's dark.

(Suddenly the lights come up, on stage and throughout the theatre. The stage is completely bare.)

PRISCILLA'S VOICE: Finally! The lights came on!
NATALIE: It must have been a power failure. I'm going to turn out the house lights. *(She exits where she entered.)*
PRISCILLA'S VOICE: I'm coming down. I hope they don't go out again. I'll clean up here tomorrow.
NATALIE'S VOICE: Careful on the stairs. Two of the steps are rotten. I almost fell last week.

(The house lights go out. The stage remains bathed in a hazy light.)

PRISCILLA'S VOICE: You mean last year. You haven't gone up there in months.

NATALIE'S VOICE: Months, you say! How you exaggerate!

(The two enter simultaneously from opposite sides. PRISCILLA has a feather duster in her hand. She is dressed like NATALIE. NATALIE carries the lighted lamp. They cross the stage without looking at each other.)

PRISCILLA: And you accuse me of playing the grande dame.

NATALIE: Besides, being down under the stage is much worse with all the rats there.

PRISCILLA: Birds of a feather flock together.

NATALIE: At least they listen to you when you talk to them. Even though they don't have to.

(They leave the stage exiting on opposite sides.)

PRISCILLA'S VOICE: Now I understand why there are more of them all the time. Instead of killing them you're inviting them to tea so they'll sit around and talk with you.

NATALIE'S VOICE: That's better than watching the neighbor's television with binoculars.

(They enter from opposite wings wearing rags on their feet to polish the floor. As they talk, they cross the stage back and forth in straight lines.)

PRISCILLA *(Without her feather duster)*: Me? Watch television? Prove it.

NATALIE *(Still carrying the lighted kerosene lamp)*: One day, when I catch you, I'll take your picture.

PRISCILLA: I don't know what camera you'll use.

NATALIE: Well, I'll make it a watercolor.

PRISCILLA: An oil painting would be better.

NATALIE: I'll turn out one of those still lifes they hang on pub walls.

PRISCILLA: That wouldn't surprise me, with the way you love wine.

NATALIE: I may love wine but you, like any good bourgeoise, are hooked on chartreuse.

PRISCILLA: Look at the proletarian! Her father was a landowner.

NATALIE: I should say so. He owned half of the county when he died. The other half my mother bought to have for her own hideaway.

PRISCILLA *(Jumping back to their earlier conversation)*: When you were in that dressing room, what happened?

NATALIE *(Picking up their earlier talk)*: Everything is the same, just the same. It even felt...as if I could smell Nestor.

PRISCILLA: My dear, he certainly had a strong odor, but after twenty years!

NATALIE: I know that, but with my nose I could sense him.

PRISCILLA: What you sensed is your hunger for a man.

NATALIE: Has it been twenty years...or twenty-two?

PRISCILLA: You kept poor Nestor a martyr.

NATALIE: And you kept him a virgin.

PRISCILLA: Twenty-two...or twenty-three?

NATALIE: The thing is, it smells as if he had been there yesterday.

PRISCILLA: Wasn't yesterday Wednesday?

NATALIE: More or less.

PRISCILLA: Wasn't Dr. Nazario supposed to have come?

NATALIE: Most likely he's having an attack of amnesty again.

PRISCILLA: Yes, I'm sure he said Wednesday.

NATALIE: Poor man, each day he's worse.

PRISCILLA: It's amnesia.

NATALIE: What?

PRISCILLA: He has amnesia, not amnesty.

NATALIE: Well, that's even worse.

PRISCILLA: Of course, since he's over eighty...

NATALIE: I'll put some mothballs on him.

PRISCILLA: He said he was going to bring the new script.

NATALIE: That way, at least, the clothes will be protected.

PRISCILLA: Or did he say Friday?

NATALIE: Friday?

PRISCILLA: Maybe you would rather smell mothballs than Nestor.

NATALIE *(Stopping)*: Aren't you tired?

PRISCILLA: This is good for the circulation.

NATALIE: Friday we must put the files in order.

PRISCILLA: Why?

NATALIE: If Dr. Nazario is going to come...

PRISCILLA: We can leave the files until next week.

NATALIE: Again? You thought up some kind of an excuse not to do it last Friday.

PRISCILLA: An excuse? What about your rheumatism?

NATALIE: I don't have rheumatism. It was only that my back hurt. Everyone gets a backache. I read about it in a magazine. But it was you who —

PRISCILLA: Anyway, would you like me to confess something to you?

NATALLIE: If we start letting down our guard...

PRISCILLA: Who's talking about letting down our guard?

NATALIE: What's this thing you're going to confess to me?

PRISCILLA: You can't give me any lessons about —

NATALIE: It wouldn't be that you were playing around with your own husband on me...

PRISCILLA: I suspect that we'll never find it.

NATALIE: What? The script?

PRISCILLA: Yes, I've been thinking about it for a long time.

NATALIE: Is that your confession?

PRISCILLA: Someone did some poking around in the files, didn't they?

NATALIE: When?

PRISCILLA: I'm talking about back then...some weeks ago.

NATALIE: Some weeks ago we started poking around, ourselves.

PRISCILLA *(Starting to clean again)*: Everything was messed up.

NATALIE *(Starting to clean again)*: It never was very organized.

PRISCILLA *(Pointing to a lamp that NATALIE is still carrying)*: Where are you going with that?

NATALIE *(Looking at the lamp)*: I was just saying that my arm was getting tired. *(NATALIE exits.)*

PRISCILLA: You know very well why it was never really organized.

NATALIE'S VOICE: Yes, because you were in charge of it.

PRISCILLA: Whatever I arranged by day, Nestor messed up at night, not to mention the pamphlets. *(Mimicking someone.)* "Could you keep these pamphlets until Tuesday? Naturally, comrade." And where were they to be kept? Well, in the files! Where else, if not there? With everything turned upside down and having to be started over again. For that kind of job, there's always Priscilla. She's no actress, nor is she a political activist. A traveling companion, oh yes, she's that. She's only the director's wife. True enough, and she's the one, naturally, who shoulders the debts. *(She stops.)* Speaking of debts, I'm going to take this opportunity to call an emergency meeting of the Board of Directors. *(Pause.)* Good. The meeting will now come to order. We'll have a reading of the agenda. The first and only item: immediate payment of the city tax. The Treasurer's report: the current lack of funds compels us to sell the toilets on the second floor, inasmuch as those on the first floor were sold last year. We grant authority for this purpose to the man who is our legal consultant and advisor, Dr. Nazario. *(Pause.)* The proposal is unanimously approved. *(She resumes her cleaning.)* Questions and requests.

NATALIE *(Enters, still cleaning but without her lamp)*: Are you sure today is Thursday?

PRISCILLA: Yes. Now, let's hear the requests.

NATALIE: Okay. Lend me your brown coat.

PRISCILLA: You're planning to go out now?

NATALIE: Who told you I wanted to go out?

PRISCILLA: Well, if not, why do you want my brown coat?

NATALIE: Because I'm changing the lining in mine.

PRISCILLA: The lining? Again? Would you mind telling me what you do inside that coat?

NATALIE: It's none of your business. Will you lend it to me? Yes or no?

PRISCILLA: So, you are going out.

NATALIE: Oh, come off it.

PRISCILLA: Besides, it's not brown.

NATALIE: Okay, then it's chestnut.

PRISCILLA: It's dark beige.

NATALIE: Light ochre.

PRISCILLA: Pale chocolate.

NATALIE: Just say it's brown.

PRISCILLA: Never.

NATALIE: Why do you think we'll never find it?

PRISCILLA: What? The script?

NATALIE: Yes.

PRISCILLA: I've already told you that. When we started to organize the files —

NATALIE: Everything was all messed-up. Do you realize how you're repeating yourself? That's a sign of senility.

PRISCILLA: That's because you don't get it.

NATALIE: Yes, I do. I'm going out. What's the matter?

PRISCILLA: Again? You spend your life on the street. That's how you're ruining the lining in your coat.

NATALIE: Me, spend my life on the street! Look who's talking.

PRISCILLA: So far this year, you've been out at least three times.

NATALIE: Twice.

PRISCILLA: You see that, twice. And this is only November.

NATALIE: It's November already? Who told you that?

PRISCILLA: Domitila.

NATALIE: That's some calendar you found for yourself!

PRISCILLA (*Stopping and looking down at the floor*): Listen...

NATALIE: She knows as much about months as I know about Catholic mass.

PRISCILLA (*Still looking at the floor*): Natalie.

NATALIE: And she distinguishes the seasons according to greens and garden vegetables.

PRISCILLA (*Looking at the floor*): I think...

NATALIE (*Mimicking someone*): "Madam, there are cucumbers, now that it's summer." Or the other way around: "Madam, now that it's summer, there are cucumbers."

PRISCILLA: Look how your upperclass airs are coming out.

NATALIE (*Stopping*): What did you say you were thinking?

PRISCILLA: Good breeding produces greyhounds.

NATALIE: Better to be a greyhound than a mutt.

PRISCILLA (*Pointing to the floor*): Look at this.

NATALIE: What?

PRISCILLA: Here. These holes.

NATALIE (*Crossing to PRISCILLA*): Where?

PRISCILLA: Here. Don't you see them?

NATALIE (*Bending over*): What do you want me to see without my glasses?

PRISCILLA: What do you call those things that eat wood?

NATALIE: Wood? Things that eat wood?

PRISCILLA: Yes. They make holes and tunnels.

NATALIE: Are you talking about moles?

PRISCILLA: No, dearie, something smaller.

NATALIE: Weasels?

PRISCILLA: No, smaller still.

NATALIE: Smaller? How about microbes?

PRISCILLA: Not so small. Well, it's not important. But I think they're here.

NATALIE (*Pensive*): Shrews?

PRISCILLA (*Disturbed, she examines other parts of the stage*): The floor is full of holes.

NATALIE (*Pensive*): Beavers?

PRISCILLA (*Pointing*): Look here. (*She touches the floor cautiously with her foot.*) The wood is cracking.

NATALIE (*Thinking*): Mandrills?

PRISCILLA: It must be all chewed up inside, like Swiss cheese. (*She touches another spot.*) The same thing is happening here.

NATALIE: No, not mandrills.

PRISCILLA: Are you listening to me, Natalie? (*Distressed.*) Do you realize what this means?

NATALIE (*Coming out of her zoological reflections*): What?

PRISCILLA: We've been fighting for this theatre so many years, battling one group after another, defending every corner tooth and nail.

NATALIE (*Touching her mouth*): You're right. With our teeth.

PRISCILLA: So that these creatures can come now and eat it up. And we don't even know what they're called, damn it!

NATALIE *(With determination)*: Don't worry, Priscilla. There's an easy solution. *(She exits rapidly.)*

PRISCILLA: What solution? Natalie! Where are you going?

NATALIE'S VOICE: I'm going to look at the encyclopedia.

PRISCILLA: Don't be an idiot, Natalie! Besides, we sold it three years ago.

NATALIE *(Entering, with the rags no longer on her feet.)*: Three years ago? Why?

PRISCILLA: Don't you remember? To pay to have the roof fixed.

NATALIE: What roof?

PRISCILLA: You're worse than Dr. Nazario.

NATALIE: Oh, yes! The water dripping into your room.

PRISCILLA: Dripping? There were streams pouring down on my face every time it rained. *(She takes the kerchief off her head.)* Why, one time I almost drowned.

NATALIE: That's what happens when you sleep with your mouth open.

PRISCILLA *(Pointing to the ceiling above the auditorium):* And then the house roof began to crack —

NATALIE: Of course, that's the reason you snore so much.

PRISCILLA: It's better to be a snorer than a sleepwalker.

NATALIE: Who's a sleepwalker?

PRISCILLA: No one. What happens is that you dream in relief.

NATALIE: You're saying that I'm a sleepwalker? That's slander.

PRISCILLA *(Pointing to the stage floor):* And now, with everything else, we've got things destroying the floor.

NATALIE: I've got it!

PRISCILLA: What?

NATALIE: The name of those bugs: termites.

PRISCILLA: Termites? Are you sure? How do you know?

NATALIE: It came to me, like a flash. There, the matter is resolved. So, I'm leaving. Will you lend me the coat or not?

PRISCILLA: How is it resolved? We have to do something to put an end to them. Don't you realize they're actually agents of capitalism?

NATALIE: Do you think so? As tiny as they are?

PRISCILLA: If we don't stop their feet, they could eat their way through all the wood in this building. And then it's...so long to The Ghost Playhouse!

NATALIE: We can't let that happen. There must be something more we can do. *(She stamps violently on the floor.)*

PRISCILLA: Don't! *(She restrains her.)* What are you doing? That's not the way. Do you want to ruin the stage?

NATALIE: I want to get rid of those agents.

PRISCILLA: But not that way. We've got to find a scientific method. *(She inspects the floor.)*

NATALIE: A scientific method. Of course. *(Pause.)* Do you suppose that Engels wrote something about termites?

PRISCILLA: I don't think so.

NATALIE: Because, knowing the way Marx was, I would swear that he didn't.

PRISCILLA: It would surprise me, too. He had other flights of fancy.

NATALIE: He certainly did, now that you mention it.

PRISCILLA: In any case, I would look somewhere else.

NATALIE: Dr. Nazario told me —

PRISCILLA: Closer to accepted practice.

NATALIE: And it isn't the first time —

PRISCILLA: Take for example, at the hardware store. *(She starts to leave.)*

NATALIE: Are you listening to me?

PRISCILLA *(Stopping)*: What?

NATALIE: You are certainly forgetful, my dear.

PRISCILLA: What did Dr. Nazario tell you, and what isn't the first time?

NATALIE: That they are losing hope for him.

PRISCILLLA: For whom, Dr. Nazario?

NATALIE: No, for Marx.

PRISCILLA: Because they've been considering Dr. Nazario a hopeless case for years, but now, you know —

NATALIE: It's not Dr. Nazario.

PRISCILLA: If it weren't for him, there'd be nothing left of the Playhouse, not even the foundation.

NATALIE: I'm talking to you about Marx.

PRISCILLA: He has his memory lapses, it's true, but he knows all the tricks that.... Did you say Marx? What's happened to Marx?

NATALIE: They say that he's outdated, that he hasn't been on target, not even once.

PRISCILLA: That's news!

NATALIE: That's what I say.

PRISCILLA: Such news, such common knowledge.

NATALIE: And such a way to get out of reading *Das Kapital*.

PRISCILLA: You hit the nail on the head.

NATALIE *(After a pause)*: Have you read it?

PRISCILLA: What time do they close the hardware store?

NATALIE: So, are you going to lend it to me or aren't you?

PRISCILLA: My coat? Can't you see that I'm going out?

NATALIE: What a coincidence.

PRISCILLA *(Taking off her smock)*: It's not a coincidence; it's a necessity. We have to act quickly if we don't want the termites to eat us all up.

NATALIE: What are you planning to do?

PRISCILLA: The termite is an insect, right?

NATALIE: If not, it's close to it.

PRISCILLA: Well, for insects you use insecticide.

NATALIE: Insecticide? With that awful smell?

PRISCILLA: Here we go again, you and your sense of smell.

NATALIE: Surely there's a more natural way that's less violent...

PRISCILLA *(Heading for the wings)*: Of course, using dialectics.

NATALIE: To be sure. So, have you read it or haven't you?

PRISCILLA *(Exiting)*: What are you talking about?

NATALIE *(Following her)*: Das Kapital.

PRISCILLA'S VOICE: The hardware store is going to close on me.

(BLACKOUT)

SCENE 2

PRISCILLA enters from the wings, in a housedress, dragging a blanket upon which are heaped various cardboard boxes and stacks of dusty papers. She stops in an area downstage near the apron, which is somewhat more illuminated than the rest of the set. She sniffs around the stage and rubs her nose. From her pocket she takes a handkerchief and a bottle of cologne. After drenching the cloth with the cologne she holds it up to her nose and breathes in deeply. She puts away the handkerchief and the cologne and sniffs all around once again. She exits through the wing on the opposite side, shouting.

PRISCILLA: Natalie, come here! There is almost no smell now! *(She returns immediately with a low chair, which she sets next to the blanket. She sits down and while she arranges the boxes around her she shouts again toward the audience.)* Can't you hear me, Natalie? Honestly, it doesn't smell. And there's more light than out there. *(She sniffs again, takes out the handkerchief, passes it under her nose and puts it away. She picks up some papers noticing how dusty they are.)* I forgot my gloves. Can you bring them to me? I don't want to pat myself on the back, but it was a good idea to come in here with the files, don't you think? It's brighter, more comfortable and less humid. I think those pains in your back come from being out there so many hours in that ugly little room. *(She finds an old photo.)* Look how handsome Nestor is here! *(She looks on the back.)* Richard II. Do you remember how handsome Nestor was, playing Henry of Bolingbroke? Natalie! Won't you come in here once and for all? *(She goes on looking at the photograph.)* Those stockings looked so awful on him. Purple, weren't they? They were ghastly! And then that stupid cap on his head... Of course, the poor dear was trying to cover his bald spot. *(She remains pensive.)* Sometimes I think... You know what, Natalie? Sometimes I think it was good he died. He wouldn't have known how to grow old. If he was already the way he was, at forty-something... I'm not talking about his appearance. *(She looks at the photo.)* Look at him: like a birch tree. So virile. He could outperform them all. And he was doing double duty, at that. But with his corset and the special boots for his arthritis, his premature wig and that obsession of yours about getting rid of his blackheads... *(She takes out her handkerchief and the cologne bottle and uses them again to shield her nose. She sniffs around.)* Come on. You're not going to be asphyxiated. What a mania you have about odors. It's been over a week since I put it down and the directions said three days.

(NATALIE enters in a housedress, wearing a gas mask. She carries an old cardboard box, overflowing with papers, and a stool, which she sets down rather abruptly next to PRISCILLA. She tosses some gloves on the blanket. As she exits PRISCILLA responds.)

PRISCILLA: How you overreact!

(NATALIE reenters with several folders, mostly empty. She sits down next to PRISCILLA, who, after putting on her gloves, begins to put the papers in order.)

PRISCILLA: I think separating the programs from the reviews is a mistake. The same goes for putting the photos together with the programs, and the press releases with the reviews. It would have been much more logical to put the reviews with the releases in the same spot as the programs. Then put the photos to one side with the posters. Better yet, the photos and the reviews could go in one place but next to the programs, and, in another place, the posters and the press releases but separated. Naturally, if we put the photos and the posters together, and the releases with the reviews in another place, the programs could stay to one side. The main thing is that everything should be logical. *(Pause.)* Not for us but for posterity. You'll agree to that, won't you? You'll probably tell me what posterity is going to do when they pick up a program. *(She takes a paper.)* For example, this one...and what they'll ask: "Let's see, what did the critics say about Gorki's *The Lower Depths*?"

NATALIE *(Lifting her mask for a second)*: Not a word.

PRISCILLA: Well, that proves my point. Because they could spend years and years without knowing where to look for a review that, in the end, doesn't even exist. *(Thinking.)* And why wasn't there any word from the critics? Oh, yes! We never got to open the play. It was the first time they closed the theatre down on us, wasn't it?

NATALIE *(Raising the mask for a second)*: It was the third time.

PRISCILLA: The third? What were the first two? Well, it doesn't matter. The thing is that the programs should be set apart and organized but next to the reviews, which should also be organized. Why don't you take off that mask? You look ridiculous. Besides, it won't do you any good because it's one of the props.

NATALIE *(Taking off the mask)*: To begin with, I don't know why you mix the blackheads with the corset and the wig. They have nothing to do with each other. And finally, the mask is a testimonial.

PRISCILLA: So you've come up with a testimonial!

NATALIE: Yes, I have.

PRISCILLA: And what do you want to make a statement about? That is, if I'm allowed to know.

NATALIE: It's not about; it's against. *(She fans herself with a paper.)*

PRISCILLA: Against what?

NATALIE *(Pointing to the stage floor)*: Against polluting pesticides.

PRISCILLA: Oh come on! I already told you I didn't put down pesticide; I put down insecticide.

NATALIE: Isn't that the same thing?

PRISCILLA: Do you want the termites to finish off the theatre?

NATALIE: That's better than destroying the ozone layer.

PRISCILLA: The what?

NATALIE: Didn't I say it right?

PRISCILLA: The layer of what?

NATALIE: I read it in a magazine: the layer of...what did I just say?

PRISCILLA: So, now you're reading that rubbish from the bourgeois press?

NATALIE: In any case, you're certainly going to ruin my lungs. For a month I haven't been able to set foot on the stage with that foul smell in here.

PRISCILLA: A month! I only put it down three days ago.

NATALIE *(Giving her a clipping)*: Take this.

PRISCILLA *(Without taking it)*: What is that?

NATALIE: It's the press release about *The Lower Depths*. You know that play is my weak spot.

PRISCILLA: Your weak spot goes from your head to your feet. I don't know what Nestor saw in you with so many ailments.

NATALIE: He found in me what he was looking for. *(Holding out the clipping.)* Do you want this or not?

PRISCILLA: What does it say?

NATALIE *(Putting on her glasses)*: The usual. *(She reads.)* "The Ghost Playhouse is presenting Gorki's *The Lower Depths* next Thursday at their location on Peace Street. The company will present a caustic social drama by the Russian author..." etcetera, etcetera. "The director, Nestor Coposo, that controversial man of the theatre, says that this play constitutes an indictment against..." *(She stops.)* And speaking of blackheads, why did it bother you so much, that he should get rid of them?

PRISCILLA: Bothered me?

NATALIE: The fact that I was sleeping with your husband didn't upset you, but when it came to his blackheads —

PRISCILLA *(Dryly, as she takes the clipping)*: Give it here. I'll put it with the program since there are no reviews of this, or photos or posters or anything. You know that was money lost, jobs lost. And they almost fined us. I don't know how many thousands. If it weren't for Dr.Nazario —

NATALIE *(Placatingly)*: Priscilla...

PRISCILLA *(Sarcastically)*: But, of course, to do or not to do the play was the least of it. It was about being provocative, wasn't it? Exploring the contradictions in the system and making the powers that be reveal their repressive nature with —

NATALIE *(Placatingly)*: Priscilla, listen.

PRISCILLA *(Sarcastically)*: Unless there was a good part in the play for you and you could convince him that —

NATALIE: Priscilla, please!

PRISCILLA *(After a pause)*: What?

NATALIE: I only removed them a couple of times.

PRISCILLA: What are you talking about?

NATALIE: I just said it to make you angry, but actually he only let me squeeze them out a couple of times in all those years.

PRISCILLA: Are you talking about his blackheads?

NATALIE: The truth is that it bothered him a lot that you kept after him with that...obsession, as you call it. He realized that they looked terribly ugly on him with his fair skin. On the other hand...

PRISCILLA: A couple of times?

NATALIE: Well, let's say three...or four.

PRISCILLA: Four.

NATALIE: Four, okay, but no more than that.

PRISCILLA *(Getting up and exiting to one side)*: You always have been a real perfectionist.

NATALIE: That's true.

PRISCILLA'S VOICE: What are all those folders you brought for?

NATALIE *(Spreading them out on the blanket)*: One is for the press releases, another for the programs, another for the reviews and another for the photos. All of them in chronological order, naturally.

PRISCILLA *(Entering with a roll of papers of different sizes)*: And the posters?

NATALIE: I thought they'd look really nice in the lobby.

PRISCILLA *(Putting the roll on the blanket and sitting down)*: Like an exhibit.

NATALIE: That's it: the history of The Ghost Playhouse.

PRISCILLA *(Taking a photo out of a box)*: Look who this is.

NATALIE: Who?

PRISCILLA: You, in *Antigone*.

NATALIE: Finally! *(She grabs it hastily, looks at it and tears it up.)*

PRISCILLA: What are you doing?

NATALIE: I've spent years trying to get my hands on this picture.

PRISCILLA: Why are you tearing it up? It's a historic document.

NATALIE: That's exactly why. I don't want to go down in history with those bags under my eyes...and those lips. *(She shows her a torn piece.)* Do you think this photo did me justice?

PRISCILLA *(Looking at it)*: The truth is that you were a little old for the part.

NATALIE *(Taking the piece from her and tearing it up even more)*: *Antigone* is a myth and myths don't grow old.

PRISCILLA: Myths don't, I agree, but actresses do.

NATALIE: Well. I'm younger than you are.

PRISCILLA: That's yet to be proved.

NATALIE: You're crazy! Next you'll claim I was the one who bombed the church and burned the courthouse.

PRISCILLA: Tell me it isn't awfully strange that there's no record of your birth or your baptism.

NATALIE: All right. I've had enough of that subject! Someday your old friend History will clear this up.

PRISCILLA: Either that or my buddy Archaeology.

NATALIE: What?

PRISCILLA: Nothing. Nothing at all.

NATALIE: You know what I was telling you? Well, it wasn't four times; it was five.

PRISCILLA *(Concerned)*: Five? *(Silence.)* Five?

(NATALIE doesn't answer. PRISCILLA picks up one of the boxes and exits through the side where she entered. NATALIE watches her leave out of the corner of her eye. She sniffs around herself with a grimace of displeasure.

She picks up a folder and fans herself furiously. Without stopping she gets up and examines some of the spots on the floor where PRISCILLA discovered the termites. Because of her movements some sheets of paper fall out of the folder. She picks them up and looks at them with a distracted air, but something she reads startles her and she lets out a shriek. She examines the pages with great excitement.)

NATALIE *(Murmuring)*: No...it can't be. *(She shouts.)* Priscilla! I found it! *(She murmurs.)* It can't be, but it is! It really is! *(She shouts.)* Priscilla come here! It's the script! I found it!

(PRISCILLA enters with a light brown coat and a handbag.)

PRISCILLA: What did you say?

NATALIE *(Calming down suddenly)*: Where are you going?

PRISCILLA: You found what?

NATALIE: Are you going out?

PRISCILLA: What was it you found? Speak.

NATALIE: And you talk about me. Who is it who spends her life going out on the town?

PRISCILLA: Who told you I was going out?

NATALIE: What about your coat and your handbag?

PRISCILLA: What coat, what bag?

NATALIE: And you talk about me.

PRISCILLA: I talk about you?

NATALIE: What coat, what bag, she says. What a hypocrite!

PRISCILLA: Hypocrite, she says. Look who's talking! *(Mimicking her.)* "Four, but no more than that." And then you'll see how, when all is said and done, you'll confess that your affair was no more than a blackhead orgy.

NATALIE: All right. Take a look at this and leave if you dare. *(She holds the papers in front of PRISCILLA's face.)*

PRISCILLA: What is that?

NATALIE: Oh, so now you don't know how to read?

PRISCILLA *(Being sarcastic as she reads)*: It's jealousy that clouds my... *(Startled.)* What is this? *(Incredulous, she takes the paper and reads.)* The Siege of Leningrad. It's not possible! *(She leafs through other pages.)*

NATALIE: Yes, it really is! You're going off gadding about and I've found the script.

PRISCILLA: It can't be. Where is the rest of it?

NATALIE: And you talk about me....

PRISCILLA (*Looking over the pages*): This is only the title page, the cast of characters...and a blank sheet.

NATALIE (*Showing her the empty folder*): They were in here.

PRISCILLA (*Reading*): *The Siege of Leningrad*... It doesn't seem possible.

NATALIE (*Going over to the heap of papers on the blanket*): The rest of it can't be far off. Where there's smoke there's fire. (*She searches through the folders that she brought in.*) You said we'd never find it.

PRISCILLA: It was written on his typewriter, that's for sure. It had those crooked "n's".

NATALIE: The "n's", the "l's" and the "p's"... He was partial to italics. (*Looking through the folders as she opens them.*) Empty.

PRISCILLA: And of the author, not a trace.

NATALIE (*Continuing to look through the folders*): No, nothing.

PRISCILLA: It's such a mystery.

NATALIE: Nothing: not a ghost of a trace.

PRISCILLA: Do you think it was necessary?

NATALIE: But this was a sign. (*She looks in the boxes.*)

PRISCILLA: Tell me, do you believe?

NATALIE: Do I believe what?

PRISCILLA: That it was necessary.

NATALIE: That what was necessary?

PRISCILLA: So much mystery.

NATALIE: Mystery, what mystery?

PRISCILLA: About the author.

NATALIE: What author?

PRISCILLA: The author of the play.

NATALIE: What play?

PRISCILLA: What play could it be?

NATALIE: *The Siege of Leningrad?*

PRISCILLA: What do you think?

NATALIE: What do I think about what?

PRISCILLA: What play could it be?

NATALIE: *The Siege of* —

PRISCILLA: That's enough!

NATALIE: Enough what?

PRISCILLA: I'll start again. Was it necessary to keep up so much mystery about the author?

NATALIE: That's the least of it. What was driving me crazy was everything else.

PRISCILLA: What are you talking about?

NATALIE: Everything else.

PRISCILLA: Okay. But can't you be a little more specific?

NATALIE: Well, to begin with there's the script. Do you think that you can put on a play without having the script?

PRISCILLA: Who didn't have the script?

NATALIE: Nobody. Aren't you going to keep looking?

PRISCILLA: What do you mean nobody? *(She looks through the boxes without paying much attention.)*

NATALIE: Not one of the actors. Each one had his own part, thank you. But, on top of everything else, the script was in pieces, like a jigsaw puzzle.

PRISCILLA: I don't understand you.

NATALIE: The pages had no numbers. We'd arrive one day and Nestor would give each of us one or two pages to rehearse. It was like doing a puzzle. You didn't know what went first or what came afterward.

PRISCILLA: Why was that?

NATALIE: Do think that you can rehearse a play that way?

PRISCILLA: You mean no one had the whole thing?

NATALIE: It was driving me crazy.

PRISCILLA: No one other than Nestor, of course.

NATALIE: Every day I said it to him, "I'm not a trained seal. I'm a dedicated actress and I want to know how I'm to play this character. And another thing. Those Russian names. There isn't a soul who can learn them."

PRISCILLA: But why so much secrecy?

NATALIE: Honestly, some of those names with three or four words were impossible and you had to repeat all of them each time.

PRISCILLA: Could it have been true...that business about the infiltrators?

NATALIE: "How are you, Vladimirovich Stephanikov Trilietski?" "Certainly, Comrade Vladimirovich Stephanikov Trilietski."

PRISCILLA: So much secrecy for that?

NATALIE: My role was fascinating, I think.

PRISCILLA: Tell me. Do you believe it might be true?

NATALIE: What?

PRISCILLA: That there were infiltrators in the company.

NATALIE: From the police? They were everywhere.

PRISCILLA: Who were they?

NATALILE: They were in the company, in the union and in the party. They pulled it off very discreetly.

PRISCILLA: That's why Nestor acted so strange, remember?

NATALIE: Nestor, strange?

PRISCILLA: Yes, back then...before the accident.

NATALIE: The accident?

PRISCILLA: During the final rehearsals —

NATALIE: You're calling it an accident?

PRISCILLA: He always got so hysterical before each opening night. Yet, those last few days... He seemed calm, didn't he? And so reserved.

NATALIE: I'm asking you, since when did you decide it was an accident?

PRISCILLA: I haven't decided anything, Natalie! I call it that because we can't call it anything else. Is that clear? Don't you remember we even swore to it?

NATALIE: What we swore to was not to call it murder. I remember that very well.

PRISCILLA: And if we don't call it murder nor an accident, what would you like to call it?

NATALIE: At least, as long as we can't prove it.

PRISCILLA: Prove it? What are we going to prove after so many years?

NATALIE: I remember it very well.

PRISCILLA: Is it twenty-three years? What year is it now?

NATALIE: What are we going to prove, you say?

PRISCILLA: Tell me in what year —

NATALIE: What are we going to prove? *(Sternly. She stops searching and takes off her glasses.)* Priscilla, this is very serious; it calls for a General Assembly.

PRISCILLA: What?

NATALIE: Just what you hear. I'm convening an emergency session of the General Assembly.

PRISCILLA *(Indignant)*: That's not fair! You're doing this just because I'm going out.

NATALIE: I'm doing this because there are critical symptoms of astigmatism here.

PRISCILLA: Symptoms of what?

NATALIE: Didn't I say it right?

PRISCILLA: There are no symptoms of anything here! What are you talking about?

NATATLIE: Skepticism, that's it!

PRISCILLA: Astigmatism. You're a great party member.

NATALIE: I mean skepticism. There are symptoms here of —

PRISCILLA; There are no symptoms of anything. What's happening is that I want to go out and because of that —

NATALIE: What are we going to prove, you say! Why are we looking for the script, eh? Why have we spent twenty years looking for it?

PRISCILLA: Twenty-three.

NATALIE: Why have we spent half our life buried in this theatre? Twenty-three or twenty-four years?

PRISCILLA: Half our life, she says...

NATALIE: What year is this?

PRISCILLA: You can't label me as a skeptic.

NATALIE: I meant what I said. I'm calling a General Assembly. I'm fifty percent of it.

PRISCILLA: Not you, not anybody. It was I who started it.

NATALIE: Oh really? Whose idea was it?

PRISCILLA: What idea?

NATALIE: That we should stay here living in the theatre.

PRISCILLA: Okay, it was yours…but only after I spent a month shut in here.

NATALIE: Two weeks, just two.

PRISCILLA: Putting up with the first attacks, while the rest of the company was mysteriously disappearing.

NATALIE: I didn't disappear! The police went looking for the others. You know that perfectly well.

PRISCILLA: What I know is that I was scared to death, spending that time here alone.

NATALIE: That's true, but I got here after three days.

PRISCILLA: Besides, when you think of that name: The Ghost Playhouse.

(Abruptly, NATALIE's attitude changes. Agitated she looks around worriedly.)

NATALIE: Priscilla! Where are you, Priscilla?

PRISCILLA *(Obviously annoyed)*: No, Natalie, please! Not now.

NATALIE *(Walking downstage and shouting to the audience)*: It's me, Natalie! Are you there, Priscilla?

PRISCILLA: This isn't the time, Natalie. I've already told you that I'm going to—

NATALIE *(Without listening to her)*: I couldn't get here any sooner. *(She turns and looks at PRISCILLA as though surprised.)* Oh, you're here.

PRISCILLA *(Unhappily resigned)*: Yes, I'm here.

NATALIE *(Crossing to PRISCILLA and hugging her)*: I couldn't get here sooner, Priscilla. I had to hide. It seems they've caught Felix and Roberto. How are you doing?

PRISCILLA *(Half-heartedly)*: I'm all right.

NATALIE: Yes, they got Roberto, too, though it looks like they'll let him go tomorrow. We don't know anything about Lola or Chris. They haven't come by here?

PRISCILLA *(Still half-hearted)*: No.

NATALIE: And the police?

PRISCILLA *(No change)*: Fine, thanks.

NATALIE: I asked if the police had come.

PRISCILLA: Oh yes, of course.

NATALIE: And the judge and the governor and a notary, right?

PRISCILLA: Yes, everybody.

NATALIE: And you?

PRISCILLA: Yes, me, too.

NATALIE: I asked what have you been up to?

PRISCILLA: Oh, that. I was here.

NATALIE: They've searched everything, right? *(She points up above.)* And they've taken away the railing, haven't they?

PRISCILLA: Yes, as you see.

NATALIE: And they didn't do anything to you?

PRISCILLA: No, as you can see.

NATALIE: That's a relief. According to Dr. Nazario...I spoke to him yesterday...he says that you don't have anything to worry about. He'll take care of everything...after a few days. They don't have anything against you. You're just the owner of the place...and, as Nestor's wife, but that's —

PRISCILLA *(Interrupting her)*: As his widow, you should say...

NATALIE: What...? Oh, of course. As his widow...

(They look at each other in silence. PRISCILLA, too, now acts strange.)

PRISCILLA: I am Nestor Coposo's widow and don't you forget it, Natalie. Do you understand? While you —

NATALIE: Priscilla, please. We have to stick together now. Nestor...isn't here any more. We both loved him, didn't we? And he...he loved, both of us. We can't change that. That's the way it was, and now Nestor is no longer with us. There's just you and me.

PRISCILLA: You and I have nothing in common anymore.

NATALIE: Nothing? Are you sure? What about Nestor's love? And his fight, which was ours, too? And this theatre that he gave his life for?

PRISCILLA *(Returning to her previous mood)*: Listen, Natalie. Since you're becoming so noble and rounding up these memories all by yourself —

NATALIE *(Without losing her grand air)*: We have everything in common, Priscilla. What separated us before must now unite us. His death is not the end but the beginning.

PRISCILLA: What soap opera did you get that from?

NATALIE: A war lost does not decide the battle. *(She falters.)* Or is it the other way around...? But we will march united...into the final battle.

PRISCILLA: That sounds familiar.

NATALIE: In the meantime, you know there are several cans of clams in the lounge.

PRISCILLA: What?

NATALIE: It might be a good idea for you to stay in the theatre for a couple of days, in case they try to pull a dirty trick.

PRISCILLA: Listen, Natalie —

NATALIE: And there are some anchovies. Dr. Nazario is afraid they'll take advantage of the company's disbanding to shut the place down and bury the whole affair.

PRISCILLA: Let's see if we can clear up one thing —

NATALIE: You haven't read the newspaper, have you? What filthy pigs! Only ten lines and they're full of —

PRISCILLA: Better yet, two things. First, in order to remember —

NATALIE: Although with the clams, smell them first in case they've gone bad.

PRISCILLA: I'm saying that in order to have collective memories you have to have complete agreement. And secondly —

NATALIE: There were ten lines, as I said, and they were full of lies. An accident, they're calling it.

PRISCILLA: It's one thing to remember and another to talk nonsense.

NATALIE (*With an abrupt change she shouts*): Who's talking nonsense here?

(*They look at each other in silence. Simultaneously, they glance at the boxes of papers and then straight up overhead.*)

PRISCILLA: Is it raining?

NATALIE: It seems like it.

PRISCILLA (*Looking at the boxes*): It's leaking.

NATALIE (*Looking at other boxes*): Over here, too.

(*They move over to the boxes. PRISCILLA picks up a box, the folders and the low chair. NATALIE begins to drag the blanket with the other boxes and the stool on top of it. They both cross toward the side through which PRISCILLA entered at the beginning of the scene.*)

PRISCILLA: Rats, termites, leaks...

NATALIE: Time is treating The Ghost Playhouse cruelly.

PRISCILLA: Not to mention what it's doing to us.

NATALIE: Don't tell me about it. I'm younger than you are.

PRISCILLA: That remains to be seen.

NATALIE: Weren't you going out?

PRISCILLA: Who told you that?

NATALIE: Well, what about your coat?

PRISCILLA: What coat?

NATALIE: And you talk about me...

PRISCILLA: Me? I talk about you?
NATALIE: Who's talking crazy now?
PRISCILLA *(Laughing)*: Astigmatism!
NATALIE: Well, look at what you —
PRISCILLA: I what?
NATALIE: How you carry on about a half dozen blackheads.
PRISCILLA: A half dozen? *(NATALIE doesn't answer.)* A half dozen?

(They exit. Lights down.)

(BLACKOUT)

SCENE 3

During the blackout, the music of the Russian national anthem The Internationale *can be heard. Crescendo until the lights come up to reveal several buckets and other containers placed here and there. NATALIE enters dressed to go out, carrying an enormous radio-cassette player from which the music pours forth at full volume. As she crosses toward the opposite side, she glances at some of the containers indifferently and looks upward. She exits. The music fades gradually in the distance. When it can no longer be heard PRISCILLA appears upstage clad in a housedress. She moves downstage as though drawn by a sound coming from the audience. She tries to see something in the darkened theatre, shading her eyes with her hand.*

PRISCILLA: Natalie, is that you? *(She listens.)* Are you there, Natalie? *(Getting no answer, she stops and turns to go upstage. She pauses to look at the buckets and containers on the set and then looks upward. Finally, she scans the entire auditorium, the theatre boxes, and the balconies. At last, she speaks in a low voice to an imaginary audience.)* Ladies and Gentlemen. *(Pause.)* Distinguished audience... *(She almost laughs.)* Beloved Ghost. *(Pause.)* The fact is there is no one who can save this place. *(Pause.)* Isn't there anyone who can save it? Who said that? *(Pause.)* No one. No one said it. Certainly not I. *(Pause.)* If the ship sinks, I'll go down with it. *(Pause.)* That's a metaphor, of course. Or something like that. *(Pause.)* In any case, there's still a lot of water to be crossed. *(Pause.)* There I go with another metaphor. I'd better just keep quiet. *(She turns around and heads upstage as the lights go down.)*

(BLACKOUT)

SCENE 4

During the blackout lively salsa music can be heard playing at medium volume. As the lights come up again the stage is empty except for a folding chair upstage. On it sits the radio-cassette that is playing. NATALIE enters dressed for an outing in the country. She carries a checkered tablecloth, which she spreads gaily on the floor. She stands off a little and looks at the placement, changes it slightly and exits on the side from which she entered. All her movements lightly follow the music's rhythm. PRISCILLA enters from the opposite side in clothes less casual than NATALIE's. She is carrying a basket covered with a napkin. She looks at the tablecloth, puts her basket down on top of it and changes the position of the cloth slightly. She exits where she entered. NATALIE reenters pulling a wagon loaded with flowerpots containing a variety of plants. She notices the change in the position of the tablecloth and corrects it. She sets the flowerpots down around her and observes the total effect. She shifts some of the pots and exits with her wagon where she entered. She returns at once and places the pots she had moved back in their original position. As she exits again PRISCILLA enters carrying in one hand a caged bird. In the other hand she holds a tall stand for the cage. She places it upstage and hangs the cage on it. She looks at the tablecloth and corrects its position once again. As she exits she passes NATALIE, who is carrying on her shoulder a red flag, a flagpole and a flagstand. NATALIE sets the flag up not far from the birdcage and the bird instantly starts to sing. She looks at the tablecloth and corrects its position. She exits. After a pause, both enter simultaneously, each from a different side. PRISCILLA carries a jug full of red wine. NATALIE carries a rolled up banner with a pole attached at each end. She lays it on the floor downstage. Barely looking at each other, they sit down at either side of the tablecloth. PRISCILLA puts the jug on the cloth next to the basket and begins to take out the usual country picnic food. NATALIE picks up the jug and takes a big swallow as PRISCILLA watches out of the corner of her eye. Finally, they both start to eat, nibbling here and there from different containers, taking a drink every now and then. All the while, they ignore each other, as best they can, and look with apparent interest and satisfaction at their surroundings. NATALIE shows her enjoyment especially of the salsa music. Occasionally, a small incident arises when they both reach, at the same time, for some food or the jug of wine. At times, sporadic bursts of song from the bird draw their attention. It should be obvious that they are quarreling but both are trying to avoid it with excessive indifference. At the same time, they hide their irritation with feigned happiness. After awhile, they finally begin to talk.

NATALIE *(With sarcastic gaiety)*: Well, how nice!

PRISCILLA *(Equally gay)*: That's what I say! *(Pause.)*

NATALIE: This is very well-attended.

PRISCILLA: Calling a meeting proved successful. *(Pause.)*

NATALIE: If we continue like this, there won't be enough room for all of us.

PRISCILLA: We'll have to make more space somehow.

NATALIE: Or hold the meeting outside.

PRISCILLA: Or put some people out on the street. *(Pause.)*

NATALIE: This tastes good.

PRISCILLA: The quiche is delicious. *(Abruptly she drops the piece which she just sampled back in the basket. Pause.)*

NATALIE *(With great delight she picks up the same piece)*: Of course, there's no comparison with last year's appetizers. They were sensational. *(Pause.)*

PRISCILLA *(Rummaging through another container)*: When you have croquettes you don't need anything else.

NATALIE: Your stuffed pastry shells were the hit of the party. Dr. Nazario kept on remembering them for a whole month...from his bed. *(Pause.)*

PRISCILLA: When all is said and done, the tossed salad with Russian dressing was the least important thing. Absolutely. As for ideology, there must be no shortage of that.

NATALIE: There's no salad without ideology. And vice versa.

PRISCILLA: Simple courtesy doesn't diminish valor. Would you pass me the wine for a little bit, so you don't fall asleep with it in your arms?

NATALIE *(Handing her the jug)*: I wasn't about to. If you were hankering for champagne...

PRISCILLA: For the love of God, will you be quiet? Champagne on a day like today? *(She takes a drink.)*

NATALIE *(Suddenly, in a pompous tone)*: On a day like today in the year 1886, the working class took a giant step toward the emancipation of —

PRISCILLA *(Suddenly angry):* She's lost control! No, gentlemen, she can't control herself! She's like Pavlov's dog!

NATALIE *(Also angry)*: You want lack of control? Just think of your father, a real hound dog. And for your information I can control myself whenever I feel like it!

PRISCILLA: My father never had hound dogs!

NATALIE: Whose dog did you say?

PRISCILLA: It couldn't be just a normal invitation. No, gentlemen, it had to be something to incite a class struggle.

NATALIE *(Standing up and swaying to the rhythm of the music)*: Am I controlling myself or not?

PRISCILLA *(Motioning around herself)*: Now look, not a soul.

NATALIE *(Paying no attention to PRISCILLA, she calls out to the bird)*: Hello there, Maiakowski. Do you like this music? *(The bird sings.)*

PRISCILLA *(Imitating NATALIE'S pompous tone)*: On a day like today in the year 1886, the proletariat defeated...the three egg quiche!

NATALIE *(Talking to the bird)*: The music may change but the words... Isn't that so, Maiakovski? The words...

PRISCILLA: That's it. It's the words, always the words. You see, calling the meeting together was a success! *(Standing up, she addresses the invisible speakers.)* How are you, Roberto? Why, it's you, Christina! How well you look. Oh, there's Lola... Come in, come in, Felix... Let's have a round of applause for Dr. Nazario! Here come Vincente and Ramona, the lovers from Verona! Hey there, Pepe! You brought your guitar and everything! *(Speaking to the wings.)* Easy there, calm down! Don't crowd. There's room for everybody!

(NATALIE has gone over to the radio and turned up the volume. She dances defiantly. PRISCILLA interrupts her act and, for a moment, looks at her with contempt. Finally, she walks over to the radio and turns it off. NATALIE stops her dance routine and, unperturbed, she sits down in front of the tablecloth and goes on eating. PRISCILLA does the same. They eat in silence, as though nothing has happened.)

NATALIE *(Very nicely)*: Would you please pass the wine?

PRISCILLA *(Nicely, too, handing her the jug)*: With great pleasure.

NATALIE *(Taking the jug)*: The pleasure is mine. *(She takes a drink.)*

PRISCILLA: So I see.

NATALIE: Have you tried the meatballs?

PRISCILLA: Thank you. It's enough just to smell them.

NATALIE: Nestor didn't believe in the spontaneous behavior of the masses either.

PRISCILLA: Are you saying that on account of the meatballs?

NATALIE: The revolutionary conscience, he used to say, should make the workers' movement more productive, so that their longing for emancipation and all that sort of thing won't be wasted in a spontaneous uprising.

PRISCILLA: And he told you this in bed?

NATALIE: You haven't tried the meatballs?

PRISCILLA: What meatballs? Is this what you're talking about? *(She takes a meatball and examines it closely.)*

NATALIE: What's going on now is a lot of revisionism, so whatever happens happens. That's all right, too. I'm not saying it's not. If we don't revise things, then you can't... My coat, for example: if I didn't check the lining every now and then... But, of course, you go along enjoying the coat and one day you say to yourself, why don't I redo these lapels, too? They're so big and they don't wear them like that anymore. So you change them and nothing happens and everything's really fine and you're so content. And then, another day, you see that your friends are wearing their coats shorter and you begin to see yourself as an outcast and...what if I shorten mine a little and see how it looks on me? And so you shorten it and it's fine. And the next year someone tells you that it's so wide that it looks like a big bell and she tells you that a cinched-in waist shows off your figure. So, you take it in and you look much younger. And you think that people are looking at you more and that they'll invite you to more parties and it's wonderful. Then, naturally, you think why don't you change the shoulder pads to give yourself that very modern executive look? Then, what about the color? I don't know. I look a little old-fashioned, don't I? Hardly anyone is wearing this color. What if I send it to the dry cleaner's so they can perk it up a little? And these buttons, you can hardly see them. It would be better to put on those really flashy square ones so that at parties people will notice how you, too, can be original. And the pockets? What are pockets for? To hide your hands, like some railway worker? To squirrel away the leftovers at a picnic? No, forget about pockets. And so, you go along revamping the coat from top to bottom, from inside to outside. And if you keep taking it off and putting it on... Then one nice day at one of those parties, the waiter comes up to you and says, "Madam, if you'll pardon me...your rear end is showing."

(During NATALIE'S monologue, PRISCILLA has been burying meatballs in the flowerpots.)

PRISCILLA: Okay. *(She pauses without stopping what she is doing.)* So tell me, when do you get invited to all these parties?

NATALIE *(After a pause)*: Wednesdays, darling. *(Pause.)* May I ask what you're doing with the flowerpots?

PRISCILLA: I'm planting your meatballs.

NATALIE: Oh, really. *(Pause.)*

PRISCILLA: One must plant for the future because the present is black for us. Of course, you're so young those kind of things don't worry you. I'm talking about some day in the future. You're still caught up in the insanity of the revolution, so to speak, and you don't see beyond that. I mean you don't see past the end of your nose. But since I am so old, I have to think about tomorrow because the present appears so black. *(She looks at a meatball.)* These are bad times for meatballs. The masses, poor souls, are keeping their spontaneity in check these days. You know that even Domitila, who's one of the proletariat, says that her family doesn't want to try them. I'm talking about meatballs. They all prefer hamburgers, she says. How's that for spontaneity? And just tell her that she belongs to the oppressed masses and she'll hang up her apron and leave us in the lurch. Or she'll remind us of the wages we're paying her. It's just as well that she knows what straits we're in. The other day, by the way, she told me that we eat worse than her family does. *(She buries a meatball in a flowerpot.)* In the long run, these are bad times for meatballs. I'm sure they're never served at your parties, am I right?

NATALIE *(Daydreaming)*: As long as the blockade lasts there's no hope for an improvement in food supplies.

PRISCILLA *(Turning toward NATALIE)*: What are you saying?

NATALIE: What?

PRISCILLA: That's it. What?

NATALIE: What about what?

PRISCILLA: What you just said...that stuff about the blockade and the food supplies.

NATALIE: I said that?

PRISCILLA: Now you're acting crazy.

NATALIE: Who's acting crazy?

PRISCILLA *(Imitating NATALIE)*: As long as the blockade lasts, I don't know what sort of food and how much...

NATALIE: Did I say that?

PRISCILLA: It turns out she's not just acting crazy, she is crazy.

NATALIE *(Surprised)*: It came to me like that, all of a sudden.

PRISCILLA: What? The craziness?

NATALIE: That statement. And now there's another one coming...we'll have to cut back the rations.

PRISCILLA: Don't worry. It's only senile delirium.

NATALIE: So long as we can't push back the enemy.

PRISCILLA: There's a lot going on. My father, at ninety, started speaking in Aramaic.

NATALIE: One must speak the truth, as cruel as that may be. The Bolsheviks never conceal anything from the people.

PRISCILLA: And when there was a full moon he sang psalms. What did you say?

NATALIE: What?

PRISCILLA: What did you say about the Bolsheviks?

NATALIE: How do you know it was Aramaic?

PRISCILLA: You talked about the Bolsheviks.

NATALIE: What about it? Is that prohibited now?

PRISCILLA: And those other statements: rations, the blockade, pushing back the enemy. Do you realize that?

(Both remain baffled for a moment.)

NATALIE: Do you mean that...?
PRISCILLA: Could it be that...?
NATALIE: It must be! If not, how did those lines come to me?
PRISCILLA: From another play, maybe? I don't believe... Let's see. Say them again.
NATALIE: What?
PRISCILLA: The sentences that went: As long as the blockade lasts...
NATALIE: How can I say them again? They just came all of a sudden, without thinking.
PRISCILLA: Try hard. Perhaps more will come to you and...
NATALIE: And what?
PRISCILLA: We'll come up with the key.
NATALIE: What key?
PRISCILLA: Oh, really, Natalie, you are losing it! If they give you an admissions test, you won't get into the old people's home.
NATALIE: The old people's home? Ha! How do you know what will happen that far off?
PRISCILLA: Why have we spent half our life looking for the script? Tell me that.
NATALIE: You may laugh, but I'm feeling things down here... *(She touches her lower abdomen.)*
PRISCILLA: Leave yourself alone and answer me. Why?
NATALIE *(Slyly)*: Something's happening down here.
PRISCILLA: Well, I'll answer myself: so we can find out who killed Nestor and why.

(NATALIE goes on with her mocking gestures, but abruptly her mood changes and she becomes still. PRISCILLA notices and stops talking. Both have the urge to grab the wine jug but stop when they realize their simultaneous gesture. NATALIE stands up and walks over to the red flag. She wipes her hand and mouth on it. The bird begins to sing angrily.)

NATALIE *(Speaking to the bird)*: Excuse me. There are no napkins. *(She walks downstage and lifts up one edge of the banner which she had left on the floor. She unrolls it part way without revealing to the audience the writing on it.)*

PRISCILLA: And today's party. A successful meeting. But she had to go and send out prehistoric pamphlets instead of normal invitations. *(She takes a sheet of paper from her bag and reads it.)* "Comrades, in these disheartening times of cowardly conformism, now more than ever, it is necessary to keep up the symbols of a fight which still goes on in every" —

(NATALIE throws the pole of the banner to the floor. The crash silences PRISCILLA.)

NATALIE: Well, my grandfather never spoke Aramaic. Think of that. In my family they all died with their wits about them. And with their boots on, just like Nestor.

PRISCILLA: What boots? His orthopedic ones?

NATALIE: They weren't orthopedic!

PRISCILLA: Well, they practically were. With that arthritis of his.

NATALIE: Think about this, too: if no one has come, it's not because of my invitation.

PRISCILLA: Oh, no?

NATALIE: It's because of your appetizers last year.

PRISCILLA: Naturally, it's because of my appetizers.

NATALIE: And your puffed pastry shells and the champagne... That whole thing seemed like a social-democratic cocktail party.

PRISCILLA *(Pointing to the empty stage)*: Now you see what's happening with your populist demagoguery. Not even the rats have come.

NATALIE: The rats already know. They always end up abandoning ship.

PRISCILLA: Of course, when they see that the ship is sinking. Like this one.

NATALIE: You're back to your defeatism now? This ship is not sinking. Get that through your head.

PRISCILLA: Get this through yours, Natalie. They're going to sink this ship in less than a year.

NATALIE: Now, what are you saying?

PRISCILLA: In less than a year. And it's not that I'm a defeatist; I'm defeated, just like you are.

NATALIE: Don't go off on a tangent. What's all that stuff about someone sinking this ship...in less than a year?

PRISCILLA: How long has it been since you saw Dr. Nazario?

NATALILE: I don't know. Why do you ask?

PRISCILLA: That figures. You don't concern yourself with anything practical.

NATALIE: Oh, no? Who takes the plants out for air? If it weren't for me, they would be dead of...of hydrophobia.

PRISCILLA: Well, talk with him. Let him explain it to you. Now that he's got his new dentures you can understand almost everything he says.

NATALIE: And Nestor's file, who cleaned that up?

PRISCILLA: You can understand almost everything...unfortunately.

NATALIE: It's going to sink, you say?

PRISCILLA: Go on, let him explain it to you.

NATALIE: You're not going to tell me they want to tear down the theatre. Not again!

PRISCILLA: The poor guy broke down in tears.

NATALIE: How many times over the years have they tried to do it? Four? Five?

PRISCILLA: I almost had to console him.

NATALIE *(Walking downstage to one side and pounding on the stage entrance)*: Look at that. Steady as a rock against the wind and the tide. How many times have they tried it? The last time...do you remember? Or was it the next to the last time? That little fat man from City Hall who perspired so. Do you remember? *(She imitates him.)* "This place is condemned; it's finished. It's done for." But they couldn't do it. It was as firm as a rock. Dr. Nazario wiped up the floor with them, and on their own turf. I wasn't bad either. Admit it. *(She rebukes an invisible speaker.)* "The Ghost Playhouse won't surrender. Get that through your head! Tell that to your bosses, the investors! Tell them, also, it's true: that ghost, that specter, is no longer haunting Europe. It's taken refuge here, waiting for better times! And no one can drive it out."

PRISCILLA: The parking garage will.

NATALIE: What are you talking about?

PRISCILLA: The parking garage will drive it out and us along with it.

NATALIE: The parking garage? That one they made in the town square? That's going to drive us out?

PRISCILLA: Worse than that: a ramp.

NATALIE: A ramp from what?

PRISCILLA: Not *from* what, *to* what. A ramp into the garage. Which will pass right through here.

NATALIE: A ramp for cars, right through here? Absolutely not!

PRISCILLA: For cars, for motorcycles, for trucks.

NATALIE: No, they shall not pass!

PRISCILLA: Oh, yes, they will pass! Talk with Dr. Nazario. Let him explain it to you. How long has it been since you talked to him? Oh, that's right, you spent a month making meatballs.

(NATALIE walks over to the radio and changes the cassette, holding back her anger while she talks.)

NATALIE: They've tried it so many times and nothing has happened. But you, all you want is to sour this party for me.

PRISCILLA: What I want is to have you put your feet on the ground.

NATALIE: Why? So I can get my shoes dirty with dust or mud...or shit? *(She taps her foot on the floor.)* Here! See, I've got my feet on the floor!

(At medium volume the cassette begins to play The Internationale. *PRISCILLA stands up and looks at NATALIE, who has stopped moving, though she is breathing excitedly. Both listen to the music, looking at each other, then looking at the theatre. Finally, PRISCILLA crosses to the banner and picks up one of the poles.)*

PRISCILLA: Shall we end the party in peace?

NATALIE *(Upset and angry, she turns her back on PRISCILLA)*: End it if you like.

PRISCILLA *(After a pause)*: I can't do it alone. A banner needs two people.

(NATALIE turns around, looks at PRISCILLA and crosses over to pick up the other pole. Now the writing on it can be seen. "LONG LIVE THE FIRST OF MAY". As the banner begins to unfurl the bird begins to sing. NATALIE and PRISCILLA also sing in a low voice. PRISCILLA looks at NATALIE and notes that she is holding back tears. She takes a handkerchief from her pocket and moves to give it to her but they notice, as they draw near each other, that the banner starts to sag. They give up on the handkerchief and pull the banner taut again, singing very quietly as the lights go down.)

(BLACKOUT)

El cerco de Leningrado (*The Siege of Leningrad*), Madrid, 1994.
Dir. Omar Grasso. Set design by Toni Cortés. Photo by Manuel Martínez Muñoz.

Judith Magre and Emmanuelle Riva in *Le Siège de Leningrad (The Siege of Leningrad)*. Colline National Theatre, Paris, 1997. Dir. Dominique Poulange. Photo by LOT.

Le Siège de Leningrad (The Siège of Leningrad), Paris. 1994. Dir. Dominique Poulange. Set design by Yves Bernard. Costumes by Françoise Tournafond. Photo by LOT.

ACT II

SCENE 5

Several boxes and piles of paper are in a row upstage. Downstage the four folders that NATALIE brought on stage in Scene 2 are now full. On a blanket at center stage there is another pile of paper. NATALIE, wearing glasses and acting more youthful, is putting the files in order. That is to say, she takes papers from one of the boxes at the rear, blows on them or shakes off the dust, looks them over and takes them to one or another of the folders, or places them on the pile at center stage. She works for a while in silence. When she comes across what seems to be a script or a duplicate she speaks without addressing anyone visible.

NATALIE: On the other hand, look at this one. I didn't want the part, but you insisted. *(She mimics someone.)* "Why does she have to be an old woman? In those days women gave birth starting at age thirteen or fourteen." Poor me, I was more scared than a snail out of its shell. "No, Nestor, it's not because of my age. What's happening is that I lack stage presence" But you, when you got some clever idea... *(Mimicking.)* "We'll do Mother Courage as a young person! Can you imagine the shocked reaction to that?" *(Pause.)* To tell the truth, I could never understand why that was such a shock. *(She walks over to the pile at center stage to leave the script there, but first she leafs through it.)* Now, I would be mature enough. *(She reads, playing the part.)* "The two of us will go onward alone. This winter will pass, like all the others. Let us go. Pull the cart before the snows come." *(She remains pensive for a moment, leafing through the script. Then she leaves it on the pile and returns upstage.)* Of course, we handed it over to that critic on a silver platter: "Baby Courage and Her Uncles," he called it, being very witty. To tell the truth, Nestor, I don't understand your desire to provoke everyone. Wasn't it dangerous enough that we were Reds? But no, we also had to be modern and different and... *(She finds a small book.)* Like this, for example! How about making a musical out of *The Communist Manifesto*! Who else would think of something like that? It's a good thing we got that out of your head, because if we hadn't... Considering the sense of humor that those in the Party had... That's where Priscilla handled it very well, you must admit. *(She imitates her.)* "This theatre is mine and you will not put that on here. If you want, you can go and stage it in the Cathedral." *(She goes to the pile at center stage, leafing through the book.)* Of course, the way things are today, it wouldn't be a bad idea. *(She reads, singing softly.)*
    "The government of the modern state
    is but a council which passes

on the business affairs they share
in common with the bourgeois classes."
What's hard is to put all this into poetry and make it rhyme. *(She tries
again.)*
"In the icy waters
of egotistical calculation,"
Okay, listen; this doesn't sound bad. *(She tries a few dance steps as she
sings.)*
"Submerged in the icy waters
of egotistical calculations,"
Though, I don't know. Since they say it's a thing of the past and very
outdated, it doesn't even come off as a dance number. *(She turns the pages
and reads.)* "The bourgeoisie compels all nations, lest they suffer from
extinction, to adopt for themselves the bourgeois mode of production..." *(She
reflects.)* You see how out-of-date that is? That's not the way it is now. *(She
reads.)* "And it forces them thus to bring in so-called civilization, or, in so
many words, to become themselves a bourgeois nation." A bit high-handed,
wouldn't you say? *(She leaves the book on the pile.)* I don't know. It would
need a lot of music. And without you to... *(She moves upstage but stops,
putting her hand to her abdomen.)* Oh! There it is again, that little pain. In
the same spot and at the same time. I'm ashamed to say it, Nestor, but...
Yes, that's it. It's as if...*(She holds back a little laughter.)* When I told you
about it the last time, I even had a little spotting...Yes, I know it's
impossible, but...what do you want? I'm not making it up. And not the part
about my breasts, either... *(She touches them and smiles. She talks to her
invisible person.)* What were you telling me? "The Revolution will make..."
How did that go? "The Revolution will make mothers' milk sweeter." That
part: sweeter... You are shameless. You said all that because you used to like
to suck me. *(She continues organizing the papers.)* You were very much the
dictator when it came to the proletariat, but when it came to this other...you
were more liberal than Casanova. Especially with me, because I was your
mistress. I'm sure you didn't keep after Priscilla as much as you did me. And
speaking of her, why is she so late? What if she's cheating on you with
Roberto! *(She laughs.)* That would be amusing at this point. Of course...
anyone who pursues her gets her. And though you haven't noticed it, he has
been pursuing her since... Since when? At least since *Waiting for Lefty* if not
before. And you didn't even notice. *(She finds a bundle of papers tied
together.)* What do you know: more pamphlets. *(She reads.)* "Comrades, the
days of the dictatorship are numbered..." You see, just another optimist. *(She
walks over to drop them on the pile at center stage.)* Roberto might not have

been a good actor, but as an optimist nobody could touch him. "The people united will never be divided..." And now, look at the way things are going for him. He's a cultural advisor. Of whom, of what? It's what I was telling you, remember? "Keep an eye on Roberto. He applauds for no reason." *(She continues organizing the papers.)* It was true: he used to love to applaud. He would get all worked up just clapping. He ruined his hands, remember? He'd clap in the theatre, in assemblies, in meetings. Even at funerals, like that time...when was it? Oh, yes, it was at yours. Do you remember? No, you don't. He was clapping and crying like a madman. And the Secret Police were there, seventy feet away, pretending not to see, but looking as if —

(PRISCILLA enters abruptly, dressed to go out and carrying her purse. She seems very upset and sad.)

PRISCILLA: General Assembly! General Assembly!

NATALIE: What's going on? You gave me a bit of a scare.

PRISCILLA: I'm sorry, Natalie, but it's just that I've come —

NATALIE: Don't tell me Roberto raped you!

PRISCILLA: Worse, Natalie. Worse.

NATALIE: Worse? He asked you to marry him?

PRISCILLA: I'll tell you about it in the Assembly.

NATALIE: Why in the Assembly? Can't you speak freely and tell me now?

PRISCILLA: No. I have to indulge in some self-criticism.

NATALIE: Self-criticism? To whom? I haven't done anything.

PRISCILLA: Who is self-criticism for? It's for me, myself.

NATALIE: Oh, right. *(Pointing to the purse PRISCILLA is carrying.)* What's that?

PRISCILLA: This? It's a purse.

NATALIE: I see that. Did you buy it? *(PRISCILLA doesn't answer.)* Tell me, did you buy yourself a purse?

PRISCILLA: Yes, I bought myself a purse. What did you want me to do? I was feeling so awful...

NATALIE *(Indignant)*: You felt awful, so awful that you bought yourself a purse?

PRISCILLA: More or less like that.

NATALIE *(Indignant still)*: Do you realize, Priscilla, how you're falling into the clutches of consumerism? Do you see what the market society is doing to you? *(Changing her tone.)* Is it real leather? *(She examines the purse.)*

PRISCILLA: That's what they told me.

NATALIE: How much did it cost you?

PRISCILLA: It was on sale.

NATALIE *(Becoming indignant again)*: On sale! That's the vilest trick of those filthy capitalists, bribing you by giving you little bits of added value. That's how they make you an accomplice in the exploitative relationship between management and —

PRISCILLA: That's enough, Natalie, please! Stop torturing me! Let me tell you the whole thing.

NATALIE: But it's not because you want to. With your General Assembly! On sale!

PRISCILLA: That's not the worst.

NATALIE: Really?

PRISCILLA: All right then, the Assembly. The meeting is open. The first order of business: I accuse myself of —

NATALIE: Just a minute! I have a preliminary request.

PRISCILLA: Make three, if you like. I'll see if I can calm myself down in the meantime.

NATALIE: One is enough, thank you.

PRISCILLA: Go ahead.

NATALIE: Was there one in burgundy?

PRISCILLA: One what?

NATALIE: A purse.

PRISCILLA: I don't know. I don't think... Why do you ask?

NATALIE: No reason. I withdraw my preliminary request.

PRISCILLA: Is it because you don't like the color?

NATALIE: It's all right. For you, yes.

PRISCILLA: For me, yes? What do you mean?

NATALIE: Nothing, nothing at all. Was your self-criticism because of this?

PRISCILLA: Because of the purse? Oh, come on! I was feeling so bad that I popped into the first store to collect myself, understand? And to take stock of the situation and see if I was on the right track. Because Roberto took me by surprise. You know what he's like. And the truth is, the way things are, and with time creeping up on us, I don't know where to turn. It's the same with you, isn't it? Without even mentioning Dr. Nazario, who finds every-thing blacker each day. And now with his prostate, I don't need to tell you. But I wasn't planning to buy anything, believe me. I wasn't in the mood. I only wanted to compose myself. Because, after saying yes to him, that I agreed that we should go ahead, a kind of confusion came over me. That's why I went into the store and paid and went back out on the street and saw myself with a purse on my arm. Tell me, do you really not like the color?

NATALIE *(After a pause)*: Tell him yes, about what?

PRISCILLA: Well, that's the thing. In the beginning I didn't understand him very well. His proposal, I mean. I didn't quite get it. You know what he's like; he's so...

NATALIE: So optimistic.

PRISCILLA: Yes, that's it. And he stutters as he talks when he gets all excited, like a kid. The fact is that he doesn't look bad for his age, probably because of the Japanese grafting.

NATALIE: What?

PRISCILLA: He's still good-looking, don't you think?

NATALIE: What's this Japanese business?

PRISCILLA: Japanese grafting. The thing is that I didn't understand him very well but I didn't want to look like a fool either.

NATALIE: What do you mean? That he's gone in for castrating little trees?

PRISCILLA: No, silly, it's hair. Some kind of hair grafts that the Japanese do.

NATALIE: Just what he needed.

PRISCILLA: So I said yes. I agreed that he should go ahead, that the main thing was to save the theatre. Because time was running out on us, and the ramp to the parking garage, too, and we didn't know where to turn. So, it could be a museum, why not? The idea is to save the theatre, don't you think?

NATALIE: Don't I think what?

PRISCILLA: But all of a sudden, this cloud came over me and I went into the store and then out to the street. And when I saw myself with the purse on my arm, I said to myself: what have you done, Priscilla?

NATALIE: Just what I've been saying. What have you done, Priscilla?

PRISCILLA: How could you accept that solution? The Ghost Playhouse turned into a bourgeois museum, a monument to the freedom of expression or something like that? Nestor turned into the glory of the nation, a hero of true democracy? To free ourselves from demolition we're going to accept consecration? Are you so defeated? Do you feel so old that you're going to give up like this, as if nothing has happened? After so many years of fighting are you going to hand over this place to the enemy? And, on top of that, so they can turn it into a mausoleum? Aren't you ashamed? What would Nestor think? Tell me.

NATALIE *(Ashamed)*: No...forgive me. I...I didn't know what I was doing.

PRISCILLA: What?

NATALIE: What do you mean?

PRISCILLA: What did you say?

NATALIE: Me?

PRISCILLA: Yes, you. You didn't know what you were doing about what?

NATALIE: About nothing. I got confused.

PRISCILLA: What were you confused about?

NATALIE: About you. But not anymore. It's all clear now.

PRISCILLA: What is clear?

NATALIE: Well, everything: the fact that you were bewildered when you saw Roberto with his Japanese hair and you went into a store to buy yourself that colorless, odorless, stupid purse. Aren't you ashamed?

PRISCILLA: No, I'm not, Natalie. That's not the main thing.

NATALIE: Do you know what I say to you? *(She crosses to one side of the stage.)* I'm going out to look for a burgundy one.

PRISCILLA *(Following her)*: Natalie, please. Forget the purses. This is very serious. The establishment wants to save us...and make us over into paper tigers.

(They exit and the lights go down.)

(BLACKOUT)

SCENE 6

There are still boxes, piles of papers and folders from the previous scene but perhaps a greater number of them. A ray of sunlight falls obliquely from above onto a cleared part of the stage. PRISCILLA enters pulling a cart with flower pots on it and, as she talks, she places it under the sunbeam.

PRISCILLA: No, Natalie, that's impossible. Maybe...I don't know... Something else.

NATALIE'S VOICE: What else could it be?

PRISCILLA: How should I know! Anything but that... Some glandular disorder or something like that.

NATALIE'S VOICE: Glandular disorder? Have you seen my breasts?

PRISCILLA: Hormones, that's what it is. Hormonal changes like what hens have.

NATALIE *(She enters wearing a Bolshevik outfit)*: Be so kind as to tell me what happens to hens.

PRISCILLA *(Arranging her plants)*: I don't know. Something that was explained to me in the poultry shop. *(She notices NATALIE's outfit.)* What's that you're wearing?

NATALIE *(Noticing the plants)*: What are you doing with the plants?

PRISCILLA: Where did you dig that up?

NATALIE: Why are you bringing them in here?

PRISCILLA: What's the occasion for the disguise?

NATALIE: Since when do you look after plants?

PRISCILLA: Ever since you don't take them out for a walk.

NATALIE: For your information this is not a disguise.

PRISCILLA: I bring them here to give them some sun.

NATALIE: It was in the storeroom.

PRISCILLA: Taking care of them, that's what I'm doing.

NATALIE: This is my Vera Yakubovski costume. *(Silence.)*

PRISCILLA: Do me a favor and take it off. Do you want Roberto to laugh at us?

NATALIE: I want his conscience to gnaw at him.

PRISCILLA: Why is that going to bother him?

NATALIE: Because he's a social climber and a traitor. What happens to chickens anyway?

PRISCILLA: Drop it, all right? He was only trying to help us...and save the theatre.

NATALIE: Hormones, they say...and do the hens get the urge to masturbate?

PRISCILLA: What?

NATALIE: Nothing. I want his conscience to bother him.

PRISCILLA: Do you get the urge...to masturbate?

NATALIE: When he sees me like this I want him to remember who he was.

PRISCILLA: Tell me the truth. Have you done it?

NATALIE: And think about what he is now.

PRISCILLA: Answer me, Natalie.

NATALIE: And may his Japanese hair graft fall out.

PRISCILLA: Okay. It doesn't matter to me what you do with your body, but you can rest assured of one thing: menopause is irreversible. Just like History.

NATALIE: Tell that to my ovaries.

PRISCILLA: As for Roberto, you don't have any reason to humiliate him. He only wants to —

NATALIE *(Looking down at her costume)*: Have you noticed how this fits me? Even better than back then.

PRISCILLA: In the storeroom you said? How did you dare go in there?

NATALIE: Shall I tell you the truth?

PRISCLLA: If you can.

NATALIE: It was as though someone called me.

PRISCILLA: What do you mean?

NATALIE: I was upstairs getting dressed when I heard a voice —in my head of course— saying, "Comrade Vera Yakubovski." Can you believe it? "Vera Yakubovski!" It's been years since I thought of that name. It must be like the other thing that's happening with my body: that I'm going backwards in time.

PRISCILLA: Don't start that again!

NATALIE: Well, maybe you can tell me what it could be. And don't even think about comparing me to a hen!

PRISCILLA: Okay, okay. Let's drop it. You heard a voice and then what?

NATALIE: Well, all of a sudden a vision came to me in which I was dressed like this, like Vera Yakubovski, and somebody, I don't know whether is was Felix or Pepe, dressed like a Bolshevik called me "comrade" and I did the same to him. And there were more people from the theatre and we all called each other "comrade". Including Roberto, I think. Do you hear that? "Comrade."

PRISCILLA: These days they say it's bad to use that word.

NATALIE: Not to me. It's just the opposite. So then I had kind of a jolt and I went to the storeroom. What an impression it made on me. If you could have seen it. Everything was there, covered with dust, so many years, so many plays. Everything, that is...except what we've had to sell. But almost everything from *The Siege* was there: the costumes, the props, the barbed wire, the guns, the cannon. Do you remember the cannon and how many problems we had?

PRISCILLA: I'd rather not remember.

NATALIE: Even Lola's washbasin. What a laugh, do you remember? *(Pause.)* Then I got to thinking. What's going to become of all this? *(She touches her costume.)* So I put this on. I don't know why. *(Pause.)* I'd better take it off. Are there lights in the dressing rooms? *(She exits to one side.)*

PRISCILLA: I think so.

NATALIE'S VOICE: What time is Roberto coming?

PRISCILLA: He said twelve o'clock. *(She looks at her watch.)* It's twelve-thirty. *(She has finished arranging the plants. She looks around. She walks about between the piles and boxes, picking up an occasional sheet of paper and glancing over it. She addresses NATALIE without speaking in her direction.)* It's not going to be easy to tell him this. You'll see. I don't think he'll understand it, poor dear. He had such high hopes. If you could have seen how he talked about Nestor. "Men of his stature can't remain in the gutter." It was right to take him out of there and...how did he put it? "And put him on the highway of History," or something like that. *(Pause.)* As metaphors go, that's not one of the best. Less so, when it comes to Nestor, who didn't even ride a bike. But I told you, he was very excited with his idea. *(Pause.)* He's not going to understand it, especially after I... Listen, why don't we give it a try? Are you there, Natalie? *(She listens.)* Why don't we rehearse it like we used to? Remember? I'll play Roberto and you play us...or the other way around. It's not going to be easy at this point, after he talked with the mayor, a couple of cabinet members, and I don't know who all else. He said that they were all very interested. How nice of them, don't you think? They all wanted to save The Ghost Playhouse. Of course, he also said —I don't know what— about changing the name and about specters being better off buried. Did you know that? *(Pause.)* I think they wanted to call it The Nestor Coposo Theatre Museum. A theatre museum. And what about us? Do we get put in the mummy section? I don't understand how I could have been so blind not to see their scheme: all wanting to save the Theatre and make Nestor into a saint. In the end, do you know why? Because they are afraid of us. Yes, afraid of you and me. Afraid of this pair of old dames, who will defend it tooth and nail to the last trench. *(Pause.)* That sentence came out pretty well, don't you think? I'll spring it on Roberto at an opportune moment. The last trench. *(Pause.)* Really, Natalie, why don't we rehearse a little? Do you hear me? *(She listens.)* What are you doing, if you don't mind telling me? Roberto will be arriving any minute. He should have been here by now. *(She stands thinking for a moment, then turns toward the wings opposite where NATALIE exited and pretends to talk to someone.)* Hi, Roberto. How are you? Come in, come in. It's been a long time since you were here, hasn't it? You'll find it's a real mess. That's because for some time the people at City Hall won't give us permission to fix anything up. Of course, we don't have the money to do it either. *(She stops and speaks to herself.)* No, it's better not to beat around the bush. *(She speaks again with a different approach.)* Hi, Roberto. We have to give you some bad news. You can take that little idea of yours and shove it. *(She stops and talks to herself.)* Okay, that's not so good either. *(She talks again using another approach.)* After thinking over the pros and cons of your proposal, as well as its relationship within a socio-political context of conflicting forces and objective conditions springing from the new world order... *(She stops and speaks to herself.)* Deadly. Suppose I approach him in a more personal vein. *(She speaks to him in a different manner.)* You know me, Roberto. And you know that I have always chosen what works best for me. But I stand by my mistakes, even though I must pay for them with a whole life of...of... Well, you understand me.

(NATALIE appears from the side where she exited. She is now dressed in a youthful, light-colored outfit that is long and filmy in the style of the early twentieth century. She is hiding something behind her back. She stops for a moment to listen to PRISCILLA.)

And you understand that, if once, a long time ago, I was able to overcome that momentary confusion, now that I'm old...or rather mature... Now that I'm a mature woman, I must be true to myself, to my principles and to Nestor. I must tell you once again: No, Roberto, I can't.

NATALIE *(Interrupting her)*: Hear, hear… What about the other moment when you were confused?

PRISCILLA *(Startled)*: Oh! What a scare you gave me! *(She looks at NATALIE's outfit.)* What are you up to now? Are you planning to go on playing with disguises?

NATALIE *(Spreading out her skirt)*: Lorca's *Doña Rosita, the Spinster.* Act One. Doesn't this fit me like a glove?

PRISCILLA: Do me a favor and get dressed the way you usually do. He's about to arrive.

NATALIE: What was it that happened so many years ago?

PRISCILLA: Nothing! Nothing happened! Do you understand? I'm an honest woman, an honorable woman with a good head on my shoulders. I know how to resist the songs of the siren and I don't need to invent miracles to carry the fight to the finish.

NATALIE: Do I invent miracles?

PRISCILLA: Besides, if I wanted to think I was somebody, I would dress up as…as Rosa Luxemburg.

NATALIE: Do I think I'm somebody?

PRISCILLA: And if the ship sinks, I'll go down with it

NATALIE: Well, I don't know whether History will be…how did you put it? Oh yes, irreversible. That's it: I don't know about History, but menopause… Look! *(She shows her a bloody sanitary napkin.)* Look how beautiful my period is.

(Before PRISCILLA recovers from her shock a bell rings offstage.)

PRISCILLA *(Reacting)*: It's Roberto! Get changed immediately! *(She exits.)*

NATALIE *(Exiting on the opposite side)*: Not Luxemburg! Rosita, the Spinster!

(BLACKOUT)

SCENE 7

On the darkened stage the sounds of demolition or construction machinery can be heard. For a few moments they could be mistaken for the sounds of war. The boxes and piles of papers are still on the stage but in different places. There are also various pieces from an old stage set that suggest a war scene: sand bags, barbed wire, guns, boxes of ammunition. In the faint light as the scene opens, one can imagine that it is taking place in a combat zone. The illusion fades as soon as NATALIE enters, dressed in a nightgown, carrying a lighted oil lamp.

With the unmistakable appearance of a sleepwalker she crosses the stage, sidestepping the obstacles in her way. A few seconds after she exits she returns upstage, and walks downstage in the same way. One notices that her eyes are closed. Nevertheless, when she gets to the apron, she stops, wavers a minute, turns around and heads upstage to a different spot. As she is about to exit she stops. She stretches one arm upward and speaks in a strangely expressionless voice.

NATALIE: Be careful, Nestor. Watch out. Get away from there, quickly. The railing is broken and you don't know it. There's hardly any light up there, so do be careful. One false step, with your arthritis...or a push by someone...who knows by whom? There is so little light up there and the railing is broken... Since when? You're going to fall. Be careful. You're going to fall headfirst, don't you remember? You're going to crack your head, Nestor, and there won't be anyone here to give you a hand or call the doctor. We're not going to find you until tomorrow, don't you remember? And there won't be a thing we can do. It'll be too late. And then it's good-bye to next week's opening of *The Siege of Leningrad...* Good-bye to the opening, good-bye to The Ghost Playhouse, good-bye to all our plans, our dreams. Everything. Good-bye to making mothers' milk sweeter, you devil. Do be careful, don't go any farther. Move away. Don't go on. The railing is rotten. Watch out. One false step, one push by someone, someone who doesn't want... What? The opening is a week from now, but it won't happen. Not now, if you die, if you crack your head, if you fall, if the railing gives way. Get away from there. Be careful, Nestor. One false step...it's so dark...or a push by someone who... Who? He doesn't want what? *(In the last statements her neutral attitude has become vaguely agitated. After a brief pause she screams.)* Watch out, Nestor!

(She disappears quickly upstage. The pounding of the machines increases in intensity. After a pause PRISCILLA enters from the wings wearing street clothes and carrying the bird in its cage. She crosses the stage with a rather furtive air, looking all around. As she starts to exit on the opposite side, the bird begins to sing cheerfully. PRISCILLA quiets it with a vigorous hiss. She exits.)

(BLACKOUT)

SCENE 8

Few things have changed from the previous scene, only the lighting, which is now more intense. The pounding of the machines continues nearer at times and with brief interruptions. PRISCILLA enters from the side dressed in unusual elegance. In her arms she carries a plastic container, which seems rather heavy. She puts it on the floor with evident relief. She rubs her arms and looks around the stage and the audience. Finally, she heads upstage with determination, picks up one of the boxes full of papers and empties it unceremoniously on the pile at center stage. As she stands, provoked, looking at the mess she has made, she appears momentarily sorrowful. She recovers and carries on the job with greater resolve, carting the other boxes the same way while muttering unintelligible sentences. To the chaotic pile she adds the files which were carefully laid out on the apron. Somewhat upset when she finishes, she seems to waver once again at the sight of a poster which she rescues from the pile. She casts aside her doubts and walks over to pick up the plastic container. She opens it and, as she empties the contents onto the pile of papers, she is interrupted by NATALIE's insistent voice, coming possibly from the audience.

NATALIE: Stop or I'll shoot!

(PRISCILLA stops moving and turns around to see NATALIE, who is indeed threatening her with a rifle. She is wearing the Bolshevik costume.)

PRISCILLA *(Scornfully)*: What are you going to shoot? That's a stage prop.
NATALIE: I wouldn't be so sure. Leave that jug on the floor.
PRISCILLA: It's not a jug. It's a can.
NATALIE: All the more reason. On the floor with it or I'll shoot.
PRISCILLA *(Dropping the can on the floor)*: Don't fool with that thing. Guns are the work of the devil.
NATALIE: That's why I said it.
PRISCILLA: All we need now would be to end up on the crime page of the newspaper.
NATALIE: Better there than on the society page. "Self-immolation is coming back in style."
PRISCILLA: Who's talking about burning herself up?
NATALIE *(Approaching, with the gun no longer aimed at her)*: Oh, no? What, then, were you about to do?
PRISCILLA: I was just going to burn down the theatre.
NATALIE: That's what you say now. How about the other day when you got all tragic?

PRISCILLA: Who me? Tragic? When?

NATALIE: The other day after Roberto left. *(Parodying PRISCILLA.)* "Let's end it once and for all. We're just a couple of old relics. Everyone else has given up."

PRISCILLA: I said that?

NATALIE: And more.

PRISCILLA: What I said was that we were acting ridiculous.

NATALIE: That, too.

PRISCILLA: And that a dignified ending was worth more than an exit in fits and starts.

NATALIE: What about when you began to shout, "Fire! The fire of purification!"?

PRISCILLA: I said that?

NATALIE: You screamed it.

PRISCILLA: It was because of the chartreuse.

NATALIE: What chartreuse?

PRISCILLA: The bottle that Roberto brought us.

NATALIE: I didn't even taste it.

PRISCILLA: I was only referring to the theatre.

NATALIE: That's what you say now. The other day...

PRISCILLA *(Defiantly)*: You're right. The other day I wanted to put an end to it all. Even to us. So what? Wouldn't that be the best thing? Burn down the theatre with us inside and end it for good? Teaching the world and that whole bunch of deserters a lesson about —

NATALIE: A lesson about what?

PRISCILLA: About what? A lesson about what?

NATALIE: Yes, a lesson about what? About pyrotechnics?

PRISCILLA: Well, let's see. Did you listen to Roberto?

NATALIE: From A to Z.

PRISCILLA: And you understood what he said?

NATALIE: Completely.

PRISCILLA: That surprises me because you never took your eyes off his hair.

NATALIE: Well, I understood.

PRISCILLA: Oh, you did? You got it all?

NATALIE *(Noticing the messed up papers)*: Why in the world did you do this?

PRISCILLA: Do you think it's worth the trouble?

NATALIE *(Looking at the papers)*: So many years, so much work...

PRISCILLA: Is it worth it to go on putting up with the guy?

NATALIE *(She continues looking at the papers)*: With the way everything was arranged.

PRISCILLA *(Looking at the papers)*: All arranged, yes.

NATALIE: Of course it's worth continuing.

PRISCILLA *(Still looking at the papers)*: I wouldn't say so much.

NATALIE: Now, more than ever.

PRISCILLA: We were never going to find it.

NATALIE: We had one sole objective: to resist.

PRISCILLA: Oh, yes? Resist? With those "tanks" working all day until night-time? With the town bureaucrats coming down on us like vultures every other day. With the businessmen dividing the world up in little pieces? Not to mention the dribble of the repentants dirtying up the carpets.

NATALIE: Which ones? You don't mean the ones in the lobby.

PRISCILLA: And then there's that other thing, that business of yours.

NATALIE: Of mine?

PRISCILLA: Yes, that thing that is happening to you. What's going to become of you?

NATALIE: Of me?

PRISCILLA: Yes, you. What's going to happen to you when you turn into a little girl?

NATALIE: I don't understand you.

PRISCILLA: I'm sure you haven't stopped to think about that. You haven't a brain in your head.

NATALIE: Don't start insulting me, okay?

PRISCILLA: Each day you'll be getting younger while I, on the other hand, will surely end up dying in a nursing home. And you? Have you stopped to think about it? Who will take care of you when you're a little girl?

NATALIE: I hadn't thought of that.

PRISCILLA: You see how you don't think things through.

NATALIE: I don't know... But I could go...to an orphanage, for example.

PRISCILLA: An orphanage! Do you know what you're talking about?

NATALIE: What about it? I don't see much difference between an orphanage and a nursing home.

PRISCILLA: You don't? It's the difference between heaven and hell.

NATALIE: Anyhow, that's a long way off. And, in the meantime —

PRISCILLA: In the meantime, what?

NATALIE: Can you picture it? To be young again?

PRISCILLA: Sure, and with pimples.

NATALIE: What pimples?

PRISCILLA: You don't remember? You said you had acne until you were twenty-eight years old.

NATALIE: Until I was twenty-eight?

PRISCILLA: That's what you told me.

NATALIE: Well, I don't care about the pimples, but to be young. Can you imagine?

PRISCILLA: To be an anarchist again...and then a hippie...and then a Catholic? How dreadful!

NATALIE: Okay, but first I was an unabashed communist!

PRISCILLA: But with pimples.

NATALIE: They have some miracle creams now.

(A deafening noise is heard offstage. After the last few minutes of silence from the machines it is all the more noticeable.)

PRISCILLA: Do you hear that? Nobody can stop them.

NATALIE *(Determined)*: Oh, no? Art will stop them.

PRISCILLA: What art?

NATALIE: What art do you think? Ours, our dramatic art.

PRISCILLA: Of course, Natalie, and before you get to the orphanage they'll be taking you to the insane asylum.

NATALIE *(Starting to drag the blanket with the pile of paper on it toward one side)*: Dramatic art, Priscilla. The theatre. We're going to act again. The Ghost Playhouse is coming back to life. *(Looking at the blanket.)* Help me, please. We'll open the theatre and act again, Priscilla. You and I. Especially me, of course, but you'll have a little part, too. You weren't doing so badly before you got married. We'll look for some really revolutionary works, especially monologues. There must be some. We'll see if they dare tear down a live theatre, a theatre that is performing. Because we will perform, you'll see. We'll open wide the doors so the public can come in. Free, if necessary. And if there is no public, as Roberto says, we'll let in the forgotten people. Every day there are more of them. You'll see how it will work. Of course, we'll get Nestor back out of the trench, but we won't set him on any highway. We'll put him out in the lobby. A photo of him, a really big one... Or a bust, which would look very nice, don't you think? Without his glasses, naturally. And I...

(PRISCILLA has listened in astonishment to NATALIE's rambling speech and has casually tried to interrupt. As NATALIE exits still talking, PRISCILLA stops and notices a handful of papers lying off the blanket on the floor. Subdued, she bends over to gather them up.)

NATALIE'S VOICE: I'll be the leading actress, of course. Almost the only one. That's the only way! We won't have to deal with the temperament of a star. We surely don't need that. Artistic temperament leaves an unpleasant bourgeois aftertaste, as Nestor used to say. I'll do monologues, but of supporting roles, including roles of the proletariat. Even though they're out of style.

(As PRISCILLA examines the pages she is stunned and falls to the floor in a faint.)

We'll look for young authors. There surely must be some, and we'll explain to them what the proletarians were. And we'll tell them about the time when they were exploited and there was a war between the classes. And imperialism, fascism and all the rest. And we'll ask them to write plays about that. Especially monologues. And some little bit part for you. And we'll also tell them that some of the characters can be called "comrade this" and "comrade that". That's not a bad thing to say if it comes from the heart.

(NATALIE enters with the red flag and the flagstand. Not seeing PRISCILLA she stops.)

NATALIE: Priscilla, where are you? Are you going to leave me here talking like...? *(She sees PRISCILLA lying on the floor and is frightened. She runs over to her.)* Priscilla! What happened? *(She drops the flag and flagstand on the floor and, in her distress, tries to get PRISCILLA to sit up.)* Please, Priscilla! What's wrong? Are you sick? Don't tell me something's come over you? No, please! Not now! Priscilla don't leave me alone in all this chaos!

(Without opening her eyes PRISCILLA stretches out the arm in which she holds a bunch of papers.)

Oh, you gave me such a fright. I thought that...

(PRISCILLA sits up halfway. She remains seated on the floor, leaning on NATALIE, still stretching out her arm.)

What came over you? Did you faint or something? *(She notices the papers.)* What have you got there?
PRISCILLA *(With a hoarse, almost inaudible voice)*: The Siege...
NATALIE: What are you saying?
PRISCILLA *(Somewhat more clearly)*: The Siege of Leningrad...
NATALIE *(Startled, speaking in a whisper)*: No...
PRISCILLA: Yes...
NATALIE: *The Siege...* No.

PRISCILLA: *Of Lenigrad.* Yes.

(NATALIE reaches out to take it with something like veneration. PRISCILLA refuses to let go. They go on clutching it and staring at it in silence.)

NATALIE *(Starting to read in a low voice)*: "Act One. The set reveals a half-destroyed fortification, next to the Kirov factory on the outskirts of Leningrad. Upstage left there is a nest of machine guns. Along the right side and part of the apron runs a trench. Upstage right, the barrel of a long range cannon rises to a great height."

PRISCILLA: Imagine. The cannon...

NATALIE: Yes...*(She goes on reading.)* "Here and there are sandbags and boxes of ammunition. A thin layer of dirty snow covers almost the entire set. As the curtain rises dawn is breaking. Fiodor Vasilievich, clad in a heavy jacket and ski mask, is cleaning his rifle. Ivan Maximovich appears from the nest of machine guns, rubbing his gloved hands together to combat the cold."

PRISCILLA *(Interrupting)*: Remember those poor fellows in the last rehearsals how they were sweating?

NATALIE: Tell me about it.

PRISCILLA: Who were those two?

NATALIE: I'm not sure... The one with the ski mask, I think, was Pepe. It must have been him, judging by his big head.

PRISCILLA: Go on. Go on.

NATALIE *(She returns to her reading)*: "To combat the cold Fiodor Vasilievich looks at him for a moment and turns back to" —

PRISCILLA: Hey! How come you're reading without your glasses?

NATALIE: You'll see. *(She continues reading.)* "And turns back to his work. Ivan Maximovich crosses to upstage right, looks off into the distance and goes over to Fiodor. He looks toward the audience and speaks without addressing anyone. Ivan: Is there some movement off there? Fiodor does not answer. Ivan: No, I'm sure there isn't. They know they don't need to move. They don't even have to fire a shot.

(The sound of the machines becomes evident again. The lights slowly go down on the two women.)

"They know that the cold and hunger will be the end of us. Fiodor, without stopping his work: If it were only that. Ivan: What do you mean? Fiodor: If it were only a question of the cold and hunger finishing us off."

(BLACKOUT)

SCENE 9

In the darkness the vibration of the machines has increased noticeably. As the lights come up the noise ceases abruptly. In contrast, it takes awhile to hear the voice of NATALIE as she continues reading the manuscript. It is nighttime and the stage is dimly lit. The set looks the same as the previous scene, except PRISCILLA and NATALIE are sitting on some bags and boxes next to each other. Behind them the red flag is upright in its stand.

NATALIE: "They slowly exit upstage without looking back. Dimitri Krotkov remains on stage covering the body of Andrei Kachurin with a blanket. He stands up with difficulty, leaning on his crutch and, expressionless, he looks around. Vera Yakubovshi enters with her military kit. Vera: Let's go, Comrade. The truck is about to leave. Dmitri doesn't answer. Vera: What are you looking at? There's nothing here of ours, any more. Remember what Andrei said? The defeated are strangers in their own land. He didn't think that moment would arrive, but that moment has arrived. Lucky for him he couldn't see it. Dimitri: He couldn't see it, but he dreamed it. Vera: What was it he dreamed? Dimitri, after a pause: The end of our dream. Dimitri and Vera look at each other. In the distance, the music of a Nazi hymn grows gradually louder. Quick curtain."

(The reading is over. NATALIE and PRISCILLA look at each other in silence, as depressed as they are astonished. At last PRISCILLA reacts and takes the script from NATALIE's hand. She leafs through the final pages and mumbles as she reads the ending. NATALIE gets up. Walking mechanically, she exits to one side.)

PRISCILLA: It isn't possible. My head is screwed on straight. I'm not a historian but my mind is sharp. I know that Leningrad didn't fall, nor did Moscow, nor the Soviet Union. The Nazis didn't win the war, did they? *(She notices that NATALIE is not there.)* Natalie! The Nazis didn't win the war and Leningrad didn't surrender, right?

NATALIE *(Entering)*: I could swear they didn't.

PRISCILLA *(Leafing through the manuscript again)*: But then, how is it possible that...? Where did you go?

NATALIE: To the bathroom. I couldn't hold it any longer.

PRISCILLA *(Giving NATALIE the manuscript)*: Now that you mention it, I can't either. *(She exits on the same side.)* But how is it possible that in the play...?

NATALIE *(Leafing through the manuscript)*: The author doesn't have his name on here either. Did you notice? The mystery continues. In any case, he couldn't have been that poorly informed...no matter how anonymous he chose to be. Maybe we misunderstood it. No, it's very clear. The betrayal of Commissar Sokolov, the scene with the German banker, the part about the Black Market. It's all very clear. And the final defeat.

PRISCILLA *(Entering)*: It's clear? Are you sure? That scene about the Orthodox priests sodomizing the boys in the Youth Group, do you understand it?

NATALIE: Well, I confess the thing gets a little complicated there.

PRISCILLA: A little, she says.

NATALIE: It must be something symbolic, but...

PRISCILLA *(Taking back the manuscript and looking through it)*: I'd say the whole thing is very symbolic. Too much so. For example, Andrei says, *(She reads.)* "We are not defending a city under siege, Dimitri, nor a country being threatened. Not even a system. What's at risk here is hope, the hope of all the doomed people on the earth."

NATALIE: That's beautiful, isn't it?

PRISCILLA: And Dimitri answers him, "Yes, Andrei. But to keep that hope alive we must make our way across the ice on Lake Ladoga. Over an icy cap whose depth no one knows, which hides unfathomable chasms and which could, at any moment, break up...under the weight of temptation." *(Pause.)* Are you aware of that?

NATALIE: Yes, I am aware. *(Pause.)* But I don't know of what.

PRISCILLA: There's the problem.

NATALIE: What problem?

PRISCILLA: The play isn't about the siege of Leningrad.

NATALIE: No?

PRISCILLA: No, it's not about World War II. It's a play with a message.

NATALIE: Yes, that's very obvious.

PRISCILLA: It's symbolic, but in a strange way.

NATALIE: Really? It's as if —

PRISCILLA: As if, what?

NATALIE: As if...

(They gaze at each other in silence.)

PRISCILLA: No, it's not possible.

NATALIE: Of course not.

PRISCILLA: Not what?

NATALIE: What we were just about to think. No, absolutely not.

PRISCILLA: It's not, right?

NATALIE: It's like a sign...or a warning. Think about it!

PRISCILLA: Or a prophecy. No, it can't be!

NATALIE: Not at all.

PRISCILLA: Certainly not.

NATALIE: What kind of mind would think that up?

PRISCILLA: It's impossible.

NATALIE: I refuse to think about it.

PRISCILLA: Me, too.

NATALIE: Rejected unanimously.

PRISCILLA: Who, then, would suppose?

NATALIE: Exactly, who would imagine?

PRISCILLA: It's been so many years.

NATALIE: When everything was so...

PRISCILLA: Nobody.

NATALIE: Nobody would even suspect it.

PRISCILLA: All that power...

NATALIE: Which seemed eternal.

PRISCILLA: And we were so sure...

NATALIE: Half the world...

PRISCILLA: Or more. All so convinced...

NATALIE: The truth was so obvious.

PRISCILLA: Yes, it hit you right between the eyes.

NATALIE: We felt so united...

PRISCILLA: We were all so young...

NATALIE: Including you.

PRISCILLA: And it seemed so near...the final battle.

NATALIE: Just around the corner.

PRISCILLA *(She returns to the script)*: No, it isn't possible...

NATALIE: It even seemed as though the general strike —you remember— would be just a matter of days and weeks.

PRISCILLA *(Leafing through the pages)*: At that time nobody could have imagined...

NATALIE: I made myself a darling, red dress, very low cut, for the occasion.

PRISCILLA *(Continuing to look over the script)*: Who could have written this?

NATALIE: It ended up being moth-eaten, of course.

PRISCILLA: Tell me, Natalie. Who do you think?

NATALIE *(Resolutely)*: No, Priscilla, a thousand times, no.

PRISCILLA: You really don't think so?

NATALIE: Nestor wasn't capable of writing...even a postcard.

PRISCILLA: He had no patience.

NATALIE: He was an actor, director, producer, yes. But a writer...

PRISCILLA: He wasn't deceitful.

NATALIE: To write this play he would have to have been a fortune-teller.

PRISCILLA: Nestor, a fortune-teller? Hah!

NATALIE; Or a defeatist. That's worse.

PRISCILLA: Nestor was very critical but he was not a defeatist.

NATALIE: Just the opposite. It was always like...like he was looking ahead to the future.

PRISCILLA: And another thing: that kind of play, back then, was...explosive.

NATALIE: Explosive? Why?

PRISCILLA: Doesn't your back hurt?

NATALIE: What about my back? I can't even feel it.

PRISCILLA: It was like a bombshell, Natalie. Can you imagine telling our troops that the other side was going to win?

NATALIE: That's true...and vice versa.

PRISCILLA: What do you mean, vice versa?

NATALIE: Why, telling the other side that our troops were going to lose.

PRISCILLA: Of course. That left them with no burning conflict.

NATALIE: You ruined the whole business for them.

PRISCILLA *(Looking over the play)*: It was a bombshell, all right...for both sides.

NATALIE: It couldn't have been. They would have made the author pay for it with...

(She grows silent. She looks at PRISCILLA, who stares back, frightened. They both look upward toward the place where NATALIE had pointed during her sleepwalking monologue. Almost simultaneously they let out a piercing shriek.)

PRISCILLA and NATALIE: Nooo!

(At the scream they both stand up. In the silence they hug each other brusquely. The embrace seems to calm them down.)

PRISCILLA: What's happening to us? Didn't we know this all along?

NATALIE: Not everything. We didn't know who, nor why. No, we didn't know everything.

PRISCILLA: And now? Do we know it now?

(The muffled roar of the machines begins to sound.)

NATALIE: Listen, those things are starting up again.

PRISCILLA: Tell me, do we know it now?

NATALIE: Some people broke the railing. Others gave him a push.

PRISCILLA: What are you saying?

NATALIE: It won't be long until dawn.

PRISCILLA: Do you hear me, Natalie? Do we know it? Could it have been some of us...or the other side?

NATALIE: Both sides, just like good friends... Shall we go to bed?

PRISCILLA: Didn't we know it...all along?

NATALIE: Of course. *(She takes the manuscript from PRISCILLA.)* And when we put the play on they'll know it, too. And they'll know what we know.

PRISCILLA: We'll put it on? *The Siege of Leningrad?* Where? How?

(NATALIE doesn't answer. She is looking out at the audience.)

NATALIE: Because they will come to see it, I'm sure. Their curiosity won't be able to stand it. They'll be dressed-up and radiant. All the same color. Both sides joining together, just like good friends.

PRISCILLA: Don't start talking nonsense again, Natalie. They're going to knock all of this down.

NATALIE: We'll see if they dare, when the theatre is full.

PRISCILLA: I'm talking about now, within a few weeks. With those machines. Don't you hear them?

NATALIE: I'm talking about now, too, this very morning. We'll go out to the street, the two of us, and start a demonstration. Can you picture it?

PRISCILLA: Not very well, to tell the truth.

NATALIE: We'll have red bandanas and carnations and a poster that says, for example —

PRISCILLA: For example: "Senior citizens of the world, unite."

NATALIE: No, dear. For example: "Now it is up to us."

PRISCILLA: Up to whom?

NATALIE: To those of us who have no regrets, or something like that. You'll see how many people will follow us. And then, right away, we'll stage *The Siege.*

PRISCILLA: Who is this "we" who is going to stage it? You and I alone? *(She walks over to NATALIE and takes her arm.)* Come on, let's get some sleep. It's very late.

(They head toward the wings.)

NATALIE: "The two of us will go onward alone. This winter will pass, like all the others. Let us go. Pull the cart before the snows come."

PRISCILLA *(Stroking NATALIE's hand)*: Goodness, how smooth your skin is getting.

NATALIE: It really is, isn't it?

(They exit. The noise of the machines grows louder, An inexplicable breeze makes the red flag wave.)

(BLACKOUT)

CRITICAL REACTION TO THE PLAY

The Siege of Leningrad "uses a metaphor: a theatre in ruins, threatened with destruction.... When the action begins, the theatre director has died, Moscow has fallen, the Communist doctrine has crumbled.... The play is thus an elegy that laments the end of a society in which Priscilla and Natalie as young women shared political ideas, a man's love, and theatrical activity."

Lorenzo López Sancho
ABC (Madrid), October 1994

"The Ghost Playhouse is about to be destroyed, turned into a parking lot. Natalie and Priscilla are living their last days of shared memories.... They dream of the past, of republics, of revolutionary wars, of class struggle.... [Sanchis Sinisterra] as an accomplished artist, juggles the signs of uncertainty, sorrow and subtle humor."

Michel Cournot
Le Monde (Paris) 1997

"In consistently comic tone, [*The Siege of Leningrad*] lays to rest the Marxist dream and lays bare a long-hidden truth." The two elderly women "set out together to search for 'The Siege of Leningrad,' the lost manuscript of a play that had never been performed. Once they find the manuscript...it reveals...what they, as committed militants, would have preferred not to know."

Gilles Costaz
Les Échos (Paris), May 1997

"*The Siege of Leningrad* says we must vindicate the best socialist ideas. I feared that the message wouldn't interest anyone; but there has been an enormous response. When we can present constructive theatre, in the sense of posing problems and saying, perhaps ingenuously, that we have to keep fighting to defend ethics and solidarity... people will support us."

Omar Grasso, Argentinean director
Primer Acto (Madrid) 1994

The Siege of Leningrad "is located at the unexpected intersection of two currents: intimate theatre and political theatre. A third tradition links the other two: the *mise en abyme* of the play-within-the-play."

Franz Johansson
Scherzo (Paris), October-November 1997

60

ABOUT THE TRANSLATOR

Mary-Alice Lessing graduated from Smith College where she spent her junior year at the Colegio de Mexico studying Mexican literature and archaeology. She received a BA from Smith College and an MA in Spanish Literature from Middlebury College. She also holds the MA in Spanish (Option in Translation) from Rutgers, The State University of New Jersey. She taught Spanish and French for twenty-three years in the Princeton Regional Schools system. During that time, she was awarded two grants from the National Endowment of the Humanities to pursue Francophone Studies at CUNY and Hispanic Studies at Princeton University. Since retirement, she has translated two plays: *Blackout*, (*Oscuro total*), by the noted Cuban-American playwright Matías Montes Huidobro, and *Vanzetti*, a play about the famous Sacco-Vanzetti trial written by the well-known Spanish playwright Luis Araújo. *Vanzetti* has been published by the ESTRENO Collection of Contemporary Spanish Plays.

TRANSLATOR'S ACKNOWLEGMENTS

I would like to express my gratitude to José Sanchis Sinisterra for granting my request to translate his play. I am extremely grateful, also, to Phyllis Zatlin and Marion Peter Holt for their thoughtful suggestions and their assistance with historical references, and to the Dirección General del Libro, Archivos y Bibliotecas of Spain's Ministry of Education, Culture and Sports for their generous support of this translation project. I wish to thank Kerri Allen for her assistance in editing and formatting the play for publication. Finally, I am thankful for Sanchis Sinisterra's creation of the two lovely, somewhat befuddled, elderly actresses in the play; it gave me such pleasure to hear them come alive as I interpreted their voices in English.

M.-A. L.

ESTRENO: CONTEMPORARY SPANISH PLAYS SERIES

No. 18 Sebastián Junyent: *Packing up the Past* (*Hay que deshacer la casa*)
Translated by Ana Mengual. 2000.
ISBN: 1-888463-10-4

No. 19 Paloma Pedrero: *First Star & The Railing* (*Una estrella & El pasamanos*)
Translated by Rick Hite. 2001.
ISBN: 1-888463-11-2

No. 20 José María Rodríguez Méndez: *Autumn Flower* (*Flor de Otoño*)
Translated by Marion Peter Holt. 2001.
ISBN: 1-888463-12-0

No. 21 Juan Mayorga: *Love Letters to Stalin* (*Cartas de amor a Stalin*)
Translated by María E. Padilla. 2002.
ISBN: 1-888463-13-9

No. 22 Eduardo Galán & Javier Garcimartín: *Inn Discretions* (*La posada del Arenal*)
Translated by Leonardo Mazzara. 2002.
ISBN: 1-888463-14-7

No. 23 Beth Escudé i Gallès: *Killing Time & Keeping in Touch* (*El color del gos quan fuig & La lladre i la Sra Guix*)
Translated by Bethany M. Korp & Janet DeCesaris. 2003.
ISBN: 1-888463-15-5

No. 24 José Sanchis Sinisterra: *The Siege of Leningrad* (*El cerco de Leningrado*)
Translated by Mary-Alice Lessing. 2003.
ISBN: 1-888463-16-3

ORDER INFORMATION

List price, nos. 1-11: $6; nos. 12-24 & rev. 6, $8.
Shipping and handling for one or two volumes, $1.25 each.
Free postage on orders of three or more volumes, within United States.
Special price for complete set of 24 volumes, $115.

Make checks payable to ESTRENO Plays and send to:

ESTRENO Plays. Dept. of Spanish & Portuguese
Rutgers, The State University of New Jersey
105 George St.
New Brunswick, NJ 08901-1414, USA

For information on discounts available to distributors and to college bookstores
for textbook orders, and for estimates on postage outside the United States,
contact:

E-mail: estrplay@rci.rutgers.edu
Phone: 732/ 932-9412 extension 25
FAX: 732/ 932-9837

VISIT OUR WEBSITE:

www.rci.rutgers.edu/~estrplay/webpage.html